PM

THE PLATONIC METHOD ⊄ AN INTERPRETATION OF THE DRAMATIC-PHILOSOPHIC ASPECTS OF THE MENO

JEROME ECKSTEIN

GREENWOOD PUBLISHING
CORPORATION - NEW YORK

Library of Congress Catalog Card Number: 68-58747

The Platonic Method Copyright © 1968 by Jerome Eckstein

All rights reserved. No portion of The Platonic Method *may*
be reproduced, by any process or technique, without the
express written consent of the author and publisher.

Printed in the United States of America

Greenwood Publishing Corporation   211 East 43rd St., New York, N.Y. 10017

TO MY BELOVED CHILDREN:
SANDRA, MICHAEL, AND ESTHER

CONTENTS

PREFACE 9

THE PLATONIC
METHOD 13

NOTES 87

MENO 93

PREFACE

THE USE OF THE TERM "METHOD" in the title of this essay, in spite of its reference to the "dramatic," might suggest a mechanized process which completely excludes surprise and diversity from its outcome. Coleridge and Descartes, for example, consider method and groping to be opposites [as illustrated in Justus Buchler's, *The Concept of Method* (New York: Columbia University Press, 1961)]. Yet it is not always the case that methodic activity is routine and its results predictable in all important specifics (in contrast to Bentham's view, as Buchler shows), and it certainly is not true of the Platonic method.

There are, as Buchler notes, "regulatory methods" and "exploratory methods." Regulatory methods are "concerned primarily with regularizing the irregular or the unregulated" (*ibid.*, p. 18). Their purpose is to achieve some type of standardized result, and they are most relevant in technology and various forms of social policy. Exploratory methods, on the other hand, attempt to create that which is "as significant for its uniqueness as for its archetypal character" (*ibid.*, p. 18). Their purpose is to produce invention, and they are most relevant in theoretical, artistic, and moral pursuits.

Plato's method is exploratory and magnificently inventive, and therefore the strong sense of groping in Plato's work is not unexpected. Groping is not necessarily a sign of weakness in method. As Buchler writes (*ibid.*, pp. 85-86):

> *No inventive process can be said to obviate groping on the part of those who engage in it. For every direction is vague in some degree when it starts with the prospect of uniqueness and unknown value in the product. Method that promises invention is query— the human effort to make the interrogative temper bear fruit. A good method for query does not mechanize effort; it only permits imaginative power to take form. Nor does it necessarily minimize effort; it only makes more likely greater substance in the reward. Method by itself cannot abolish the recalcitrancies of existence. Descartes' faith notwithstanding, no method opens a door through which one need only enter. Method does not provide*

*a way already made but part of the equipment to
devise a way. The best methods attempt to fight
vagueness of direction, but not to simplify query.
Were there nothing hidden in query, the interrogative
temper would be a jest, and each method would be a
surd or miracle. Groping, therefore, far from being,
as some philosophers believe, the sign of weakness in
a man or a method, is the price that the finite creature
is naturally obliged to pay in the process of search.*

Plato's dramatic method is especially equipped to generate the exhibitive and active functions of utterance. All modes of judgment—active, exhibitive, as well as assertive—are capable of functioning methodically. And all modes of judgment, not only the assertive, can be "cognitive." Unlike most commentators, I attempt to show how the exhibitive and active functions of the dramatic method are crucial to the understanding of the "cognitive" import of the *Meno*. Plato is the master of all the modes of judgment, and all are utilized in his Dialogues.

Since my exegesis is quite different from the traditional interpretation of the *Meno* (e.g., I believe that neither Plato nor the Platonic Socrates accepts the "doctrine of recollection," and I believe that Plato intends his slave-boy "demonstration" to be taken as a farce and not as a paradigm of teaching), the reader who is unfamiliar with the *Meno* is urged to study Plato's Dialogue first. He will then probably offer a stiffer resistance to my exposition.

I am grateful to M. I. Berger, Carol Evans, Aaron Kramer, John H. Randall, Jr., and the Philosophical Group of New York for reading the manuscript. Their critical reaction and their specific comments have been of great value to me. It will be obvious that I owe a great debt to the discussions, lectures, and writings of Justus Buchler and John H. Randall, Jr.

I am also indebted to Isidore Shapiro, whose wisdom and kindness helped me to better understand the complexities of human life. Last, but not least, I am thankful for the happy hours shared with my beloved companion, Sally Lawrence, which helped to make this work a product of joy.

J. E.
May, 1968

THE
PLATONIC
METHOD

PERHAPS THE CHIEF CHARACTER-ISTIC OF THE FOL-LOWING INTERPRE-TATION IS THAT IT TAKES PLATO'S DRAMATIC

FORM WITH UTMOST
PHILOSOPHIC SERIOUSNESS.

True, all agree that Plato is a great artist, but too many philosophers view his artistry as a mere embellishment of his straightforward philosophic assertions. His myths and character development are looked upon as adventitious adornment, which can be separated from the dialectic without loss of philosophic content. Popper goes so far as to accuse Plato of using his artistry to "lull the reader's critical faculties, and, by means of a dramatic display of verbal fireworks, to divert his attention from the intellectual poverty of this masterly piece of dialogue."[1]

As I see it,[2] however, Plato's artistry has a crucial and logical bearing on his philosophic themes. Throughout his Dialogues, he reveals his meanings by what his characters *do* (active judgments) and *make* (exhibitive judgments), as well as by what they *say* (assertive judgments);[3] the dramatic context pleads for an apprehension of the manner, as well as the content, of what is said and done. Plato, "the greatest dramatist of ideas,"[4] frequently conveys philosophic thought not only by "exhibitive judgment employing concepts and abstractions as its medium,"[5] but also by alternating between myth and dialectic; by interweaving myth with dialectic, "where it is neither easy nor desirable to separate the overt and the covert myth, the myth as announced and the myth as intellectually embodied."[6] Plato uses the three modes of judgment (exhibitive, active, and assertive) in order to communicate as fully as possible, for the respective powers of communication of these modes are not entirely coextensive. Wittgenstein's advice—"what can be said at all can be said clearly, and what we cannot talk about we must consign to silence"[7]—is often sound; but it may be more useful to note that what cannot be talked about might be done or made—or at least it can be said that it cannot be talked about.

Generally, the Socrates of the Dialogues is drawn by Plato as a full human being. Socrates is not merely a thinker—he also responds with emotions and actions; he is a "proceiver," and all of what he says, does, and makes obtains meaning in terms of his unique "gross proceptive domain"[8]—which is for all men their individual (distinctive), all-pervasive, and most comprehensive perspective. To understand Socrates adequately, it is necessary to perceive all his modes of judgment. When this is done, an interesting observation can be made; namely, the degree of sarcasm or illogic in Socrates' responses is in proportion to the degree of arrogance, brashness, hostility, or stupidity in his partner's judgments. Much of the illogicality in Socrates' arguments reveals contempt for his partner's obtuseness. Socrates demonstrates that he can dumbfound his partner into agreement by absurd arguments which even a neophyte in philosophy can disprove. Certainly, Plato sees through these spurious arguments.

Failure to appreciate properly the philosophic significance of Plato's dramatic approach leads, in my opinion, to much confusion and error regarding Plato's political and ethical views. H. D. P. Lee, in his Introduction to Plato's *Republic,* reports that whereas "the older generations of commentators were perhaps too apt to idealize Plato...and it is sometimes not easy to discover from them that Plato was not a good nineteenth-century liberal," more recently criticism has been sharper. Crossman, for instance, describes Plato as a reactionary who encourages the "dictatorship of the virtuous Right." Similarly, Popper finds Plato to be a totalitarian, opposed to all liberal or humanitarian ideas, and to be a utopian, quite ruthless in trying to actualize a "blue-print of the society at which we aim." Both Popper and Weldon criticize Plato for believing that politics can be made into an exact science. Lee thinks that "there is something in all these criticisms," and that "Plato has little sympathy with the kind of outlook we should call 'democratic.'"[9]

Although I would agree that there are very important differences between the contemporary national mass-industrialized democracy and the relatively simple and limited democracy of the Athenian city-state, I should argue that Plato's political position is much closer to that of a liberal (nineteenth- or twentieth-century) than to that of a totalitarian. For Plato, neither ethics nor politics can be an exact science, and this is one of the factors in his opposition to dictatorship. An appreciation of Plato's dramatic-philosophic method, I maintain, substantiates my views. The following interpretation of Plato's *Meno* and a few paragraphs from his *Republic* and *Statesman* will articulate and illustrate all of my previous points.

THE DIALOGUE BEGINS

Meno, the young Thessalian aristocrat who was trained in rhetoric by the Sophist Gorgias, opens the Dialogue. He avoids the usual amenities of conversation and abruptly asks Socrates how virtue is acquired. Meno expects, as becomes evident, a quick, short, and conclusive reply. Socrates retorts partially, *ad hominem,* that Gorgias has taught Meno the habit of answering questions in a grand and bold style, and he adds sarcastically:

> *...How different is our lot! my dear Meno. Here at Athens there is a dearth of the commodity, and all wisdom seems to have emigrated from us to you.... And I myself, Meno, living as I do in this region of poverty, am as poor as the rest of the world; and I confess with shame that I know literally nothing about virtue....*[10]

Although Socrates makes the logical point that he cannot speak about how virtue is acquired until he has determined what virtue is, it is obvious that he also responds psychologically (sarcastically) to Meno's brashness.

Meno, insensible to sarcasm, asks: "But are you in earnest, Socrates, in saying that you do not know what virtue is? And am I to carry back this report of you to Thessaly?" Socrates retorts condescendingly and somewhat boastfully: "Not only that, my dear boy, but you may say further that I have never known of any one else who did, in my judgment."[11] Now, the historical Meno is not a "boy," surely not a "my dear boy"; he is an important military leader. And Socrates is not exactly humble in his estimation that he never found anyone who knew the answer.

Socrates "nevertheless" invites Meno to offer his (or Gorgias') definition of virtue. Boldly, Meno declares: "There will be no difficulty, Socrates, in answering your question." His answer clearly reflects the Sophists' radically relativistic and subjectivistic view: "Every age, every condition of life, young or old, male or female, bond or free, has a different virtue: there are virtues numberless, and no lack of definitions of them; for virtue is relative to the actions and ages of each of us in all that we do." Socrates responds again sarcastically to Meno's unwitting arrogance: "How fortunate I am, Meno! When I ask you for one virtue, you present me with a swarm of them...."[12]

THE DISTINCTION BETWEEN DEFINITION AND EXAMPLE

Socrates then explains that he is searching for the common and essential traits of virtue, not for the specific differences in various kinds or instances of virtue. In short, he is seeking a definition. He illustrates by showing the inappropriateness of defining "bee" through references to the different characteristics of various kinds of bees. And Meno says that he understands. Socrates reiterates the distinction with regard to virtue and asks Meno if he understands this, too. He replies: "I am beginning to understand; but I do not as yet take hold of the question as I could wish."[13] There is not a trace of arrogance in Meno's statement, and not the slightest sarcasm or antagonism in Socrates' response to it. Oh, perhaps Meno is a bit slow-witted; but, on the other hand, it is not easy to overcome a habit of thought on the first or second exposure to its faultiness.

Socrates simply, patiently, offers three other examples of the distinction between a definition and an illustration, and asks Meno once more to define virtue. Meno says, "I cannot help feeling, Socrates, that this case is different from the others," and Socrates asks, "But why?"[14] Surely there is no impudence in Meno's avowal, nor much petulance, if any, in Socrates' rebuttal. Meno is weakening, and perhaps he is somewhat aware of it. He flees the perilous arena of logic and seeks respite in the realm of feeling. Socrates, still calmly, makes his point through another argument, and Meno seemingly understands.

MENO YIELDS A DEFINITION OF VIRTUE

At last, but still rather reluctantly, Meno gives the following definition: "If you want to have one definition of them all, I know not what to say, but that virtue is the power of governing mankind." Now Socrates can use his famous method of testing the adequacy of a definition. He suggests that Meno's definition would be inapplicable to the virtue of a slave or child. Meno agrees. Furthermore, Socrates obtains Meno's unquestioning assent to the addition of "justly" to "governing" in the latter's definition. Regrettably, Meno not only assents, but adds: "for justice is virtue." This affords Socrates the opportunity to counter, "Would you say 'virtue,' Meno, or 'a virtue'?" Meno can say only, "What do you mean?"[15] Obviously (to all but Meno), Socrates is alluding to the now tiresome distinction between a definition and an illustration; yet, he does not become irate in the face of Meno's philosophical ineptitude.

Instead, the master tranquilly proffers yet another example. The result of this effort is Meno's assertion, "there are other virtues as well as justice." Tirelessly, Socrates comments: "Yes, Meno; and again we are in the same case: in searching after one virtue we have found many, though not in the same way as before; but we have been unable to find the common virtue which runs through them all." Meno replies: "Why, Socrates, even now I am not able to follow you in the attempt to get at one common notion of virtue as of other things." Socrates responds: "No wonder; but I will try to get nearer if I can...."[16] Amazingly, Socrates' response displays only a slight sharpness; he has not yet become exasperated. He is probably less irritated by the "conceitlessness" of Meno than he would be by a display of conceitedness.

Very composedly, Socrates again elucidates the old distinction in connection with the example of "figure," and, taking another tack, encourages Meno to essay a definition of figure—for "the attempt will be good practice with a view to the answer about virtue." But Meno is loath to comply, and urges Socrates to try. The latter consents only on condition that Meno shall then present a definition of virtue. Socrates fulfills his promise with the hope of returning immediately to the investigation of virtue; but he tenders a weak definition ("Figure is the only thing which always follows colour") in order, I believe, to evince his disdain of Meno's intellect. Directly afterward, he says: "Will you be satisfied with it [let's come back to virtue], as I am sure that I should be, if you would let me have a similar definition of virtue?" The philosopher definitely would not be content with a similar definition; he would eagerly manifest its weakness through the Socratic method. Even Meno criticizes the definition, but, typically, he does it poorly. He says: "But if a person were to say that he does not know what colour is, any more than what figure is—what sort of answer would you have given him?"[17] Yet the real difficulty with the definition is the ambiguity and vagueness of "follows," not the meaning of "colour."

Socrates makes a most interesting confession in his response:

> *I should have told him the truth. And* if he were a philosopher of the eristic and antagonistic sort, *I should say to him: You have my answer, and if I am wrong, your business is to take up the argument and refute me.* But if we were friends, and were talking as you and I are now, I should reply in a milder strain and more in the dialectician's vein; *that is to say, I should not only speak the truth, but I should make use of premises which the person interrogated would be willing to admit. And this is the way in which I shall endeavour to approach you* ....[18]

With the explicit disclosure that Socrates reacts strongly and defensively to contentiousness or antagonism and mildly and logically to sincere or friendly discourse, the previous observations to the effect that the degree of sarcasm or illogic in Socrates' responses is proportionate to the degree of arrogance or stupidity in his partner's judgments receives added support. Moreover, Plato reveals that although dedicated to objective and dispassionate teaching, Socrates is conscious of his tendency to respond emotionally in specific kinds of situations. The great teacher, indeed knows himself; he knows his limitations. I am surprised that the important implications of Socrates' confession for the interpretation of the Dialogues have been generally overlooked.[19]

The master presents another, a better, definition of figure; but Meno, unmindful of his promise, requests a definition of color. Clearly Meno is stalling, and Socrates notes this. The Thessalian again promises a definition of virtue, provided that Socrates first satisfy his latest request. After a brief and charming byplay between the two characters, Socrates asks if Meno would like an answer in the familiar manner of Gorgias. Meno is delighted with the prospect, and gratified with the effect; he finds Socrates' definition of color "admirable." Socrates observes that Meno's pleasure results from familiarity with this mode of response, but he, Socrates, thinks that the second definition of figure is a better definition than that of color. And, indeed, it is. Evidently, in order to revert to the problem of virtue and cast disesteem on Meno's intellect, Socrates offers a poor definition of color and a weak first definition of figure.

ANOTHER DEFINITION OF VIRTUE

Meno yields; he defines virtue. "Well then, Socrates, virtue, as I take it, is when he, who desires the honourable, is able to provide it for himself."[20] Aside from the awkwardness of its expression, the definition is obviously weak because of its failure to come to grips with the essence of virtue. It is not especially helpful to substitute "honourable" for "virtue"; the one is as unsteady as the other. Socrates crushes the definition, but not entirely by fair tactics or against strong resistance. At first Meno opposes the Socratic position that all men desire good, and then he succumbs spiritlessly, without logical compulsion. In the course of Socrates' probings, Meno is pushed passively to the idea that desire is always of possession and to the conclusion that the acquisition of wealth is unrelated to virtue. But these are unnecessary concessions; for surely there are desires which are not concerned with possession, and wealth may be a necessary even if not a sufficient condition of virtue. Clearly, Meno is no logical giant. Indeed, he falls again into the old trap:

> SOC. *Then it follows from your own admissions, that*
> *virtue is doing what you do with a part of virtue . . . .*
> MEN. *What of that?*
> SOC. *What of that! Why, did not I ask you to tell me the*
> *nature of virtue as a whole? . . . And, therefore, my*
> *dear Meno, I fear that I must begin again and repeat*
> *the same question: What is virtue? . . .*[21]

Socrates' frustration tolerance is remarkably high, for Meno has not yet absorbed thoroughly the distinction between a definition and an illustration. It is no great wonder then that Socrates sometimes resorts to illogical devices in order to persuade Meno. It would be ludicrous and wasteful to attack an intellectual "pipsqueak" by cannon. In the interest of an economy of means, Socrates reserves his heavy artillery of logic for mightier warriors.

What is Meno's reply to Socrates' patient and persistent request for a definition of virtue?

> O Socrates, I used to be told, before I knew you, that
> you were always doubting yourself and making others
> doubt; and now you are casting your spells over me,
> and I am simply getting bewitched and enchanted,
> and am at my wits' end.... For my soul and my
> tongue are really torpid, and I do not know how to
> answer you; and though I have been delivered of an
> infinite variety of speeches about virtue before now,
> and to many persons—and very good ones they were,
> as I thought—at this moment I cannot even say what
> virtue is. And I think that you are very wise in not
> voyaging and going away from home, for if you did
> in other places as you do in Athens, you would be
> cast into prison as a magician.[22]

Plainly, this is an *ad hominem* attack rather than a logical reply. Plato, as dramatist, is exhibiting several diversionary tactics which are employed by the logically inept. (1) Meno blames his inability to produce a definition on Socrates' supposed unfair use of magical powers. Plato frowns on shunning responsibility for one's failures and fleeing from one's ignorance to the lulling comfort of the supernatural. But even if Socrates used witchcraft, it would not establish that Meno knows the nature of virtue; to think otherwise is to commit "the fallacy of the appeal to a red herring." (2) Meno adds that when not paralyzed by the "torpedo's shock," he feels no hardship in speaking about virtue. Meno implies that talking freely is a sufficient sign of knowledge. However, Socrates notes later that ignorance does not necessarily result in dumbness; the ignorant often pontificate with ease. Furthermore, Meno suggests that formerly his numerous and varied speeches about virtue were acceptable to all or almost all, thus implying—another common ploy—that public approval of his views is proof of their appropriateness. Yet, aside from the possibility that Meno could have spoken sensibly about virtue without being able to define it, public assent is no guarantee of aptness; to think otherwise is to resort to "the fallacy of the appeal to illegitimate authority." Plato and the historical Socrates are especially sensitive to the latter fallacy; witness their diligence in articulating the unsuitability of much of conventional morality. (3) Moreover, Meno attempts to intimidate Socrates into agreement, but even if this were successful it would not constitute favorable evidence for Meno's position; to think otherwise is to have recourse to "the fallacy of the appeal to illegitimate force." Meno issues a thinly veiled threat—Socrates, with his strange views, should beware of travelling abroad. But is it not his own Athens which in fact imprisons the historical Socrates and abets his martyrdom for his rational criticism of conventional morality?! How agonizing and hateful this is to Plato! Plato's message is clear: the Athenians are no better than the barbarians!

THE DILEMMA OF LEARNING

Socrates is not at all angered by Meno's reply. He is, in fact, quite gracious. He explains that he perplexes others only because he is utterly perplexed himself. He admits that perhaps once Meno did know what virtue is, but it seems that presently Meno does not know its nature. Socrates again offers to join with Meno in the inquiry into virtue. Meno, disarmed by Socrates' refusal to be outflanked by psychological assaults, tries another sort of diversion, a logical argument ("dilemma"). His argument, one used previously by some Sophists, is restated by Socrates:

> I know, Meno, what you mean; but just see what a
> tiresome dispute you are introducing. You argue that
> a man cannot enquire either about that which he
> knows, or about that which he does not know; for
> if he knows, he has no need to enquire; and if not,
> he cannot; for he does not know the very subject about
> which he is to enquire.[23]

The purpose of the dilemma is to divert Socrates from his resolute insistence upon a definition of virtue. Rather than continuing the difficult inquiry into the meaning of virtue, Meno seeks, in desperation, to abort it by arguing for the impossibility of any inquiry or learning. Meno's sense of helplessness is revealed by his willingness to discount the fact of his own (and mankind's) innumerable learning experiences (does he not admit learning from Gorgias?) in favor of an *argument* to the contrary. Moreover, were Meno's dilemma inescapable and therefore persuasive to Socrates, there would be an occurrence of learning. Thus, were the argument successful, it would thereby be self-defeating. Hence, the following "counter-dilemma" could be constructed, provided that an ideal rational discussion were assumed or defined as a discourse where only and always correct arguments were persuasive. Thus, if Meno's argument is correct, learning occurs; if Meno's argument is incorrect, there is the possibility of learning. Meno's argument is either correct or incorrect; consequently, learning either occurs or is possible—but it is certainly not impossible. Furthermore, Meno's argument rests on a particular conception of knowing (atomic, static, and rationalistic) which should be abandoned for another conception in order to preserve the useful distinction between learning and not learning. "Rebutting" or "slipping between the horns" of Meno's "dilemma" should also be encouraged. Understandably, Socrates characterizes the dilemma as "a tiresome dispute."

To resolve Meno's popular "quibble" or "dilemma," Socrates introduces the doctrine that learning is only remembering.

> ... *The soul, then, as being immortal, and having been born again many times, and having seen all things that exist, whether in this world or in the world below, has knowledge of them all; and it is no wonder that she*

should be able to call to remembrance all that she ever knew about virtue, and about everything; for as all nature is akin, and the soul has learned all things, there is no difficulty in her eliciting or as men say learning, out of a single recollection all the rest, if a man is strenuous and does not faint; for all enquiry and all learning is but recollection. And therefore we ought not to listen to this sophistical argument about the impossibility of enquiry: for it will make us idle, and is sweet only to the sluggard; but the other saying will make us active and inquisitive. In that confiding, I will gladly enquire with you into the nature of virtue.[24]

THE TWO "SOLUTIONS"

Socrates presents two solutions; the first is geared to the shallowness of the problem and its poser, but the second is much more serious. The first "solution" proclaims, with the seeming authority of wise men and divinely inspired priests and poets, that although men never *learn* anything, they can *recollect* everything. By admitting that learning never occurs, Socrates expects to assuage Meno; and by persuading Meno to accept "recollection" as a replacement for "learning," Socrates hopes to induce Meno to return quickly to the inquiry—of course, now called a "recollection."

Meno is appeased by this "solution," but he should

not be. His argument is that learning is logically impossible, and Socrates dodges the argument—neither offering it assent nor dissent—by stating that learning *never occurs in fact.* Certainly, both Plato and the historical Socrates, who stubbornly refuse to succumb to the tyranny of the factual, of the *status quo,* would not tolerate in the final analysis this type of "response"; for it falsely suggests, especially if it is taken as rationally relevant to the dilemma, that the endless nonexistence of a fact implies the logical impossibility of that fact.

Moreover, Socrates' dodge is self-defeating. For what is recognized must have been cognized previously, what is recollected must have been collected previously; and Meno's dilemma is left unanswered with regard to the original cognition or collection. Even if "there is no difficulty in her [the soul] eliciting or as men say 'learning,' out of a single recollection all the rest," there is a difficulty, according to Meno's argument, in explaining how "the soul has learned all things" during her immortality. It is unlikely that Socrates is ignorant of this difficulty when in the same sentence he connects the recognition directly to the cognition. Socrates' first "solution" merely postpones the problem until the next logical move, and he gauges correctly that Meno will not recognize the delaying tactic and thereby fail to make the appropriate move. Socrates, not respecting Meno's intellect, tries to dissolve, rather than solve, Meno's quibble quickly and to return immediately to the original problem of virtue. Socrates applies the principle of *talionus,* repaying one diversion for Meno's numerous diversions, and takes satisfaction in the superior effectiveness which his dodge enjoys. I believe that this "solution" of Socrates is one of condescension as well as expediency.

Socrates' second solution also makes a psychological appeal, but it suggests in addition a profound logical point. Socrates urges Meno "not to listen to this sophistical argument about the impossibility of enquiry: for it will make us idle...but the other saying will make us active and inquisitive." This can be taken as analogous to the peroration of a Knute Rockne half-time football pep-talk. But I believe that it has also a deeper significance. Socrates adopts a pragmatic position. He reckons with the consequences of opting for a belief or disbelief about the occurrence of learning, anticipating William James' understanding of the self-realization power of faith; and Socrates insists on the primacy of the universal experience of learning above any argument about its logical impossibility. He will not be "talked out" of the overwhelming reality of his experiences of learning. Rather, it is suggested that the concept of learning should be construed to accommodate the possibilities and actualities of learning and of not learning respectively. For the consequences of refusing to accommodate the above distinction between learning and not learning are disastrous; the coherency and effectiveness of experience would be deeply disrupted; the ubiquitous concern, success, and failure of persons and institutions to increase proficiency, for example, would have to be denied or unexplained.[25]

That Socrates puts no stock into his first "solution," the doctrine that knowledge is only reminiscence, receives confirmation from what follows immediately upon the doctrine's presentation.

> MEN. *Yes, Socrates; but what do you mean by saying that*
> *we do not learn, and that what we call learning is*
> *only a process of recollection? Can you teach me*
> *how this is?*
>
> SOC. *I told you, Meno, just now that you were a rogue, and*
> *now you ask whether I can teach you, when I am*
> *saying that there is no teaching, but only recollection;*
> *and thus you imagine that you will involve me in a*
> *contradiction.*
>
> MEN. *Indeed, Socrates, I protest that I had no such*
> *intention. I only asked the question from habit; but if*
> *you can prove to me that what you say is true, I*
> *wish that you would.*
>
> SOC. *It will be no easy matter, but I will try to please*
> *you to the utmost of my power. Suppose that you call*
> *one of your numerous attendants, that I may*
> *demonstrate on him.*[26]

Now, when Meno asks Socrates to teach him the doctrine of reminiscence, Socrates has the opportunity, psychologically, if not logically, to stop Meno's diversion with finality and resume the main inquiry. Socrates need merely point out that Meno hopes to learn, and thus Meno does not really believe in his sophistical argument for the impossibility of learning. But since Meno's request for elucidation of the first "solution" and his complete avoidance of the second solution reveals him characteristically unaffected by the subtlety and significance of the latter and attracted to the spectacularity and outrageousness of the former, Socrates cannot fight the temptation to develop the absurd doctrine of reminiscence and disdainfully win Meno's consent to it. Nor can Socrates resist displaying his cleverness by twitting Meno's unwitting setting of a trap in his use of the word "teach." Poor Meno! He protests, and proclaims his innocence of such intellectual subtlety; and he proves it immediately by making the same error in asking Socrates to "prove"—in other words, "teach"—his doctrine.

But why does Socrates ignore this stupid blunder? Surely, he sees it. I believe that Socrates has several reasons for deliberately entering the second instance of the same unintentional trap, relinquishing the chance to censure Meno again.[27] (1) He estimates correctly but contumeliously that Meno lacks sufficient acuity to see the trap and close it— even after it was pointed out to him only a moment earlier. (2) Furthermore, Socrates really believes that only his second solution, which takes learning as a possibility and actuality, is genuine. His first "solution"—which would contradict the second if the former's "recollection" excludes any prior learning—is a sham. He is prepared, after indulging himself in toying with Meno about "teach," to accept the entailment of learning which "prove" involves. Indeed, if he can convince Meno of the truth of the doctrine of reminiscence, then Meno should be ready to admit that not only has he hoped to learn but that he has actually learned! How

Socrates relishes irony—to demonstrate the actuality of learning by persuading Meno that learning is not an actuality! (3) Moreover, Socrates enjoys seducing Meno farther into the absurd.

THE SLAVE-BOY "DEMONSTRATION"

And how absurd it becomes! And how Meno likes it! Socrates undertakes to prove that learning is only recollecting by inducing Meno's slave-boy, who never studied geometry, to arrive at a geometrical truth. Socrates argues that he is not teaching the correct answer to the slave-boy. Socrates is only "asking him questions,"[28] he is not "telling or explaining anything to him."[29] Since the slave "could not have acquired it [the geometrical truth] in this life, unless he has been taught geometry,"[30] it must be that his immortal soul always possessed this knowledge. Hence, Socrates concludes, this geometrical truth "only need[s] to be awakened into knowledge by putting questions"[31] to the slave—i.e., by stimulating recollection. And, it is implied, this illustration can serve as an adequate model for all so-called "learning" experiences; they are all merely instances of reminiscence.

The absurdity of Socrates' demonstration arouses even philosophical neophytes to fight its claim, in varying degrees of intensity and specificity, for they sense the unfairness and inadequacy of Socrates' demonstration. The following are some objections which may be raised against Socrates' approach.

(1) The almost exclusive use of "leading questions" to the slave-boy by Socrates, I believe, evokes the strongest protest in the neophytes. Of course, every non-rhetorical question is intended to lead to an answer; but "leading question" as used here means what it does in a court of law —a question which contains the substance of the answer and suggests the expected affirmative or negative response. And if in a court of law a witness' recollection of an event observed by him is justifiably held suspect when he replies only to "leading questions," then it is downright silly to believe that the slave-boy's responses to Socrates' promptings are purely recollections of a prenatal knowledge of geometry. If anything, this is a demonstration of what Socrates here calls "teaching"; for Socrates is "telling" or "explaining" the answers. (2) But it is not even a demonstration of successful teaching (or recollection). The impression is left that without prompting the slave-boy could not reconstruct the argument, see any of its logical implications, cope with a slight variation of the problem, or apply the principle to a theoretical or practical situation. In short, he has not learned.

All the points of the preceding paragraph are buttressed by an examination of the very few questions put to the slave which are not "leading." Some of these questions are answered correctly, one is answered falsely, another elicits an "I do not understand," and yet another evokes an "Indeed, Socrates, I do not know." Of the first class, most are invitations to note a physical property of the diagram drawn on the ground by Socrates; the remainder ask for the products of 2×2, 3×3, and 4×2. When it comes to the enormous product of 4×4, Socrates apparently becomes apprehensive of the slave's ability to answer correctly and therefore poses his question in a "leading" form: "Four times four are sixteen—are they not?"[32] Toward the end of the "demonstration," when matters are slightly more complex, the slave-boy is even confused about noting a physical property. Socrates asks, "Look and see how much this space is," and the boy replies, "I do not understand."[33] The boy is more nonplussed when the challenge is somewhat greater. Thus, after Socrates "leads" the slave-boy to deny that the figure of eight is made out of a line of three (which was the boy's previous false answer), he asks the boy: "But from what line?—tell me exactly; and if you would rather not reckon, try and show me the line." And the response is: "Indeed, Socrates, I do not know."[34]

(3) Surely, the slave-boy's ability to point to some of the figure's physical features and to give the products of 2×2, 3×3, and 4×2 does not constitute "proof" of his prenatal memory or of Socrates' triumphant teaching. It is possible, after all, that the boy had opportunities to learn this skill and knowledge during the course of his earthly existence, before his fateful encounter with Socrates.

(4) Furthermore, when he replies, "I do not understand," to Socrates' request to count an amount of space, it is clearly a failure of understanding and not memory. Certainly, the boy does not mean that he has forgotten how to count; for he has been counting, and he continues to do a fairly good job of it. Rather, he refers to a lack in a kind of knowledge which cannot be reduced to recollection. (5) Moreover, how can the slave's failure to answer questions be explained in terms of recollection? Why did his potential omnireminiscence falter at these points? They *are* associated integrally with the other questions!

Because these criticisms are sensed even by novices, it is difficult to believe that Socrates—let alone Plato—is unaware of them. No; Socrates puts no stock in the doctrine of reminiscence, but he is teasing Meno farther into the absurd.

Socrates' response to the boy's admission of "not knowing" is ingenious; for, among other endowments, it cleverly tries to convert a hindrance into a furtherance. Nevertheless, the response raises additional obstacles to Socrates' "demonstration."

> soc. *Do you see, Meno, what advances he has made in his power of recollection? He did not know at first, and he does not know now, what is the side of a figure of eight feet; but then he thought that he knew, and answered confidently as if he knew, and had no difficulty; now he has a difficulty, and neither knows nor fancies that he knows.*

MEN. *True.*

SOC. *Is he not better off in knowing his ignorance?*

MEN. *I think that he is.*

SOC. *If we have made him doubt, and given him the 'torpedo's shock,' have we done him any harm?*

MEN. *I think not.*

SOC. *We have certainly, as would seem, assisted him in some degree to the discovery of the truth; and now he will wish to remedy his ignorance, but then he would have been ready to tell all the world again and again that the double space should have a double side.*

MEN. *True.*

SOC. *But do you suppose that he would ever have enquired into or learned what he fancied that he knew, though he was really ignorant of it, until he had fallen into perplexity under the idea that he did not know, and had desired to know?*

MEN. *I think not, Socrates.*

SOC. *Then he was the better for the torpedo's touch?*

MEN. *I think so.*[35]

Socrates skillfully attempts to turn the problem of the boy's failure to remember into evidence for reminiscence. He argues that the boy now correctly recollects that he did not recollect correctly before, and he is therefore better prepared to recollect the right reply to the query. The boy does not fail to remember, for he remembers that some answers are wrong; but he does not remember fully, because he does not yet remember the right answer. However, though Socrates' ploy is adroit, it skirts the problem. The enigma is the boy's hardship in remembering the right answer, which is integrally connected with other answers he correctly remembers and is not notably different from them in complexity or difficulty. It seems reasonable to expect the boy to remember the right reply to this query, which occurs in the middle of the "demonstration," with as much ease (or difficulty) as he remembers the other answers, if formerly he understood the geometrical theorem and is now simply recollecting it. On the other hand, it would be plausible to expect difficulties to arise at any point of the argument if this were a case of learning.

Socrates' response also artfully introduces replies to two earlier criticisms by Meno and craftily suggests a disparaging similarity between Meno and the slave-boy (remember Socrates' addressing Meno in the beginning of the book as "my dear boy"). It will be recalled that immediately prior to Meno's argument concerning the impossibility of learning or inquiry, to which Socrates responds partly by the "demonstration" with the slave-boy, Meno essays three psychological attacks on Socrates which go mostly unanswered. Meno charges earlier that Socrates is like a "torpedo fish, who torpifies those who come near him and touch him, as you have now torpified me."[36] Socrates claims now, with direct reference to the slave-boy but indirectly as a generality  and an allusion to Meno's earlier charge, that the "torpedo's shock" can act as a stimulant to knowledge rather than a depressant—and Meno agrees. Earlier, Meno implies that his having "been delivered of an infinite variety of speeches about virtue" signifies the genuineness of his knowledge of virtue. Now, Socrates notes, with direct reference to the slave-boy but indirectly as a generality and an allusion to Meno's earlier implication, that the ignorant man is also "ready to tell all the world again and again" of his false opinions — and Meno agrees. Thus, Socrates' response, among other functions, manages both to answer two of Meno's earlier weak criticisms and to embarrass Meno by its allusions to unflattering similarities between the positions of Meno and the slave-boy. Indeed, Plato subtly conveys the impression that Meno vaguely senses the embarrassment of his position. For in all of Meno's three replies to Socrates' "leading questions" about the advantage of experiencing the "torpedo's shock" there is a trace of uncertainty present, unlike the definiteness of his answers to nearly all other "leading questions." In these three instances Meno responds with "I think so" or "I think not." His reluctance to be absolute reflects his vague awareness that the response is contradictory to his former position. However, with regard to the second allusion, the observation that the ignorant are ready to broadcast their false opinions to the world, Meno's agreement is unqualified; this may be due to the second allusion's being more disguised and hidden. The first allusion, with its repetition of the striking and obvious metaphor of the "torpedo's shock," is difficult to miss altogether. It is quite likely that the second allusion bypasses Meno completely.

(6) Certainly, the second occurrence of Socrates entering the trap which he proudly avoids previously, goes

entirely unrecognized by Meno. Socrates asks if Meno thinks that the slave-boy would have "enquired into or learned" without the excitation of the "torpedo's shock," and Meno fails again to note that Socrates' acceptance of the actuality of inquiry and learning is contradictory to his first "solution" and the slave-boy "demonstration" which ostensibly supports that "solution." For the apparent point of the first "solution" and the "demonstration" is that learning and inquiry never occur, and the only knowing that happens is reminiscence. Only a few moments before, Socrates, himself, causes Meno's attention to focus on another instance of the same contradiction. Obviously, though Meno, the slave-boy, and all other men can remember the inane events and ideas of an eon, Socrates is confident that Meno will forget the pertinent logical point that has just gone by.

The contemptuous and farcical nature of the "demonstration" is also evident in its epilogue.

soc. *What do you say of him, Meno? Were not all these answers given out of his own head?*

men. *Yes, they were all his own....*

soc. *And this spontaneous recovery of knowledge in him is recollection?*

men. *True.*

soc. *And this knowledge which he now has must he not either have acquired or always possessed?*

men. *Yes....*

soc. *But if he did not acquire the knowledge in this life, then he must have had and learned it at some other time?*

MEN. *Clearly he must.*

SOC. *Which must have been the time when he was not a man?*

MEN. *Yes.*

SOC. *And if there have been always true thoughts in him, both at the time when he was and was not a man, which only need to be awakened into knowledge by putting questions to him, his soul must have always possessed this knowledge, for he always either was or was not a man?*

MEN. *Obviously.*

SOC. *And if the truth of all things always existed in the soul, then the soul is immortal. Wherefore be of good cheer, and try to recollect what you do not know, or rather what you do not remember.*[37]

(7) Socrates is so infatuated by his success with the absurd that he contemptuously dangles it before Meno's face. Not satisfied with having burlesqued his "demonstration" by the nearly continuous use of "leading questions," he must also elicit from Meno the idiotic judgment that Meno has witnessed a legitimate performance. And he succeeds. Meno assents to the proposition that the slave-boy's answers were all "given out of his own head," "spontaneous," and instances of pure "recollection."

A most surprising, subtle, and profound turn of the argument now occurs. From the surface of the dialogue it appears that there are again ridiculous contradictions, but a hint emerges from the depths which transforms the significance of the "demonstration."

(8) Socrates argues that since the boy did not acquire the knowledge in this life, then he must have "had and learned" it at another time. (a) But how can Socrates state that the boy "learned" geometry at any time, when this contradicts his first "solution" and the purpose of his "demonstration"? It is the fourth encounter with this contradiction or trap, and the third time that he has walked into it. (b) Furthermore, to say that the boy "learned it at some other time" implies that there was a time when he did not possess the knowledge, but this contradicts Socrates' argument that the boy must have "always possessed" it. This is the final absurdity of the section.

A SECOND VERSION OF THE FIRST "SOLUTION"

Nevertheless, it is not an absurdity. Apart from the single troublesome phrase, "had and learned it at some other time," the entire context makes it clear that Socrates is modifying his first "solution." Since Socrates introduces the new version of the first "solution" without fanfare, Meno is unaware of the change. Meno does not apprehend that, whereas the initial version of the first "solution" concerns reminiscences of prenatally acquired (learned) knowledge, the new version deals with reminiscences of eternally possessed (unlearned) knowledge. This is an important change.

Several consequences flow from the adoption of the new version which remove or mollify the contradictions noted in the objection (8), present an improved, although ultimately inadequate, first "solution" to Meno's problem, and suggest a serious side of the "demonstration" (8a, 8b). Socrates does not contradict himself; he does not maintain both the initial version (where prenatal learning occurs) and the second version of the doctrine of reminiscence (where learning never occurs). He entirely abandons the first version. It is obviously no solution. For the moment, he is clearly considering only the second version, which resembles a solution to the dilemma because it categorically denies the occurrence of learning (8b). Hence, when Socrates says that if the boy did not acquire the knowledge in this life, he must have "had and learned it at some other time," "learned" should be understood as a reiteration of "had" and not taken in its usual sense. Because in this context "had it at some other time" does not imply that there ever was a time when he did not possess the knowledge, the troublesome phrase becomes tractable. Indeed, the phrase even becomes suggestive: it heralds the synonymity between "learned" and "remembered." For shortly afterward, Socrates says, "...will it be taught or not? or, as we were just now saying, 'remembered'? For there is no use in disputing about the name."[38] Possibly, too, Socrates deliberately steps into the traps of the "demonstration" to hint at the subsequent feasible synonymity between "learning" and "remembering," as well as to express his contempt for Meno's minimal intelligence.

The alternative between learning, in its customary meaning (as different from remembering), and eternally possessed infinite knowledge bids descent to a deeper level of analysis. Pragmatically, there is no cognitive difference between the alternates' consequences. It is all the same whether man has no prenatal knowledge, or whether he has eternal knowledge of everything but forgets it all at birth; in both cases he must encounter in this life questions and experiences which will elicit from him "learning" or "remembrance." True, in this life the patterns of questions and experiences which actuate remembrance are often different from those which stimulate learning; therefore, it might be argued, there is a significant cognitive difference between the alternates' consequences. The situations which would be efficacious for remembering would not always be effective for learning. In fact, this argument would support the usual position that prenatal knowledge is absent, and militate against the doctrine of reminiscence of eternally possessed infinite knowledge; for the latter, unlike the former, does not ostensibly account for the differences between situations of learning and recollection. Hence, should the latter doctrine have even initial credibility, it would have to admit frankly to the same differences noted by the usual view in patterns of "learning" and recollection—except that the doctrine of reminiscence would insist that, despite contrary appearances, all the instances of "learning" are really instances of recollection. It would appeal to the current state of ignorance (amnesia) about the nature of recollection, in order to "explain" the observed differences between "learning" and recollection. Although scientific methodology would favor the usual view because of its superior explanatory power, nevertheless the practical consequences issuing from both positions or alternates would be the same. Pragmatically, operationally, then, the two positions are identical. I believe that on the deepest level this is a profound message which Plato intends Socrates to suggest by the ludicrous "demonstration." Some of the important consequences of this message must now be examined.

CONSEQUENCES OF THE PRAGMATIC EQUIVALENT

First, the pragmatic equivalency between the two positions signifies more than superficial synonymity between "learning" and "remembering" proclaimed by the undeveloped doctrine of eternally possessed infinite knowledge. The latter permits the possibility, if it does not suggest, that the customary view of learning is operationally different from its view; whereas the former forecloses that possibility. On this level, then, when Socrates says shortly that "there is no use in disputing about the name," no difference in saying "was taught" (or "learned") or "remembered," he is referring to the pragmatic equivalency between the two positions and not simply to the synonymity between the two terms under the undeveloped doctrine of eternally possessed infinite knowledge.

Second, the burlesque aspects of the "demonstration" now reveal their serious features. Socrates is aware of the inadequacies and absurdities of his "demonstration," and partly he wishes thereby to express his disdain for Meno's uncritical acceptance of the "demonstration." But on a deeper level—surely not for Meno's understanding—he wants to point to the pragmatic equivalence between the usual view of learning and the developed doctrine of reminiscence of eternally possessed infinite knowledge. His almost ceaseless usage of "leading questions" makes a fiasco of the "demonstration" equally whether viewed as an instance of learning or recollection. He is suggesting that both positions equally find the use of "leading questions" unsatisfactory. The "demonstration" is neither an instance of recollection nor of successful learning. Furthermore, Socrates' walking into the traps or contradictions of using the words "learning" and "enquiry" when on the surface he intends to say that learning and inquiry do not occur but are really instances of recollection, is deliberate; he wishes thereby to suggest the pragmatic equivalency between the two positions.

Plato reveals himself as a dramatist who does not resort merely to occasional verbal ironies and isolated segments or "businesses" of burlesque, but as an artist who exhibits the complexity of his thought by structural ironies and perhaps even an anticipation of the theatre of the absurd. Not only is the "demonstration" absurd, but it is also a demonstration of a legitimate variant of the *reductio ad absurdum* argument.

The *reductio ad absurdum* argument attempts to prove proposition A by demonstrating that the contradictory proposition, not-A, entails inconsistencies. Plato attempts to prove dramatically the legitimacy of the customary view of learning by demonstrating that the alternative doctrine of reminiscence, which is intended to remedy the supposed defects of the former, is pragmatically equivalent with the customary view. (Of course, this would be a strict proof only if there were no other alternatives, which has not been shown; but in the context of the Dialogue these are the only worthwhile alternatives considered.)

This raises the third, and final, consequence to be examined. If the doctrine of reminiscence of eternally possessed infinite knowledge is pragmatically equivalent to the customary view of learning, then the former cannot solve any problems which are intrinsic to the latter. Hence, the doctrine of reminiscence cannot be offered as a solution to Meno's dilemma about the impossibility of learning. Socrates' first "solution" is no solution; and there remains only his "second" solution. Such has been my argument before, and it becomes increasingly evident in the text following the extensive quotation just analyzed.

ONLY THE "SECOND" SOLUTION IS FRUITFUL

MEN. *I feel, somehow, that I like what you are saying.*

SOC. *And I, Meno, like what I am saying. Some things I
have said of which I am not altogether confident. But
that we shall be better and braver and less helpless if
we think that we ought to enquire, than we should
have been if we indulged in the idle fancy that there
was no knowing and no use in seeking to know what
we do not know;—that is a theme upon which I am ready
to fight, in word and deed, to the utmost of my power.*

MEN. *There again, Socrates, your words seem to me
excellent.*[39]

Of what is Socrates, euphemistically, "not altogether
confident"? First, he does not accept the outward form of the
myth in the "first solution," a tale which tries to support the
doctrine of prenatal learning, as a solution to the dilemma
about learning; it merely postpones the problem until the
next logical step is taken. And Socrates is confident that
Meno will not take that step. Possibly, Socrates even shapes
the myth to suggest prenatal learning because Meno can
more easily accept an account of knowledge as being learned
at some time rather than as never being learned. For Meno
never doubts the reality of learning, despite his arguing for
the impossibility of learning. Second, Socrates has no compelling reason to accept the myth in its refined form, sup-
porting the doctrine of eternally possessed infinite knowl-

edge, as solving the dilemma; for this doctrine is pragmatically equivalent to the usual view of learning. Third, Socrates rejects the various obvious absurdities of his "demonstration." It would be wrong to argue, however, that the two forms of the myth and the absurdities of the "demonstration" should have been better omitted. For they serve to demean Meno, which is of dramatic-philosophic importance; they lead to various significant considerations; they forcefully suggest that only the "second" solution is a solution, and that ultimately a pragmatic factor must enter into a complete account of knowledge.

The last sentence of Socrates' speech explicitly reiterates his confidence in the "second," the pragmatic, solution. The sentence and its context indicate that this is the point in the second of three segments of the Dialogue, from Meno's psychological diversions through the present speech, which Socrates is most eager to establish. Yet, though Socrates is convinced of the value of the pragmatic approach and is prepared to fight for it, there remains an important trace of uncertainty. True, he argues convincingly that Meno's dilemma ought not to discourage inquiry; but the dilemma does point to a universal state of inadequate comprehension of the learning process. Socrates is gnawingly aware that his solution does not give a sufficient account of the origin of knowledge; for if he could explain the learning process, he would not need to be "ready to fight" for the value of pursuing knowledge.

Meno remains true to character. He is blissfully removed from the subtleties, profundities, and difficulties of the discussion. His first response is that he feels, "somehow," that he likes what Socrates is saying. He is undoubtedly attracted to the "hoop-la" of myth and "demonstration," the sacral aura of immortality and the spectacle of a slave-boy learning geometry. Moreover, on the surface it appears that he has gained a victory over Socrates; for superficially the "demonstration" yields to the conclusion of Meno's dilemma. Meno's response is that Socrates' words seem excellent. Meno, the student of Gorgias, is moved by rhetoric rather than logic; Meno, the general, is quickly roused to join Socrates' "fight, in word and deed."

Since inquiry is justified, Socrates wants to investigate the nature of virtue; but Meno still insists that they should inquire how virtue is acquired. Socrates yields after some bantering, but only on the condition that they consider several hypotheses about the nature of virtue in order to examine their respective implications for the acquisition of virtue. Meno agrees. Socrates "first" hypothesizes that "if virtue is knowledge, virtue will be taught," and Meno says "certainly." Socrates comments that "we have made a quick end of this question," and urges "the next question is, whether virtue is knowledge or of another species?" And Meno replies: "Yes, that appears to be the question which comes next in order."[40]

But it is not; the next question ought to consider another hypothesis about the nature of virtue and its consequences for the acquisition of virtue. Socrates is truly making a "quick end" to the bargain, and shifts deftly to an examination of the nature of virtue. He finally wins this point; although, unquestionably, he would have won it earlier had he so desired. The analyses of the nature of virtue which follow are not as "quick" and superficial as that occurring in the first hypothesis, but they are not the most deliberate or profound that are possible. True, Socrates finally reflects on the implications of his analyses for the acquisition of virtue, and thus the hypothetical nature of the deliberation is not rejected. But that is perfectly in keeping with Socrates' intention from the beginning of the Dialogue when he proposes to study the "quid" of virtue before its "quale." That is what Meno persistently refuses to do throughout the discussion. Now, however, Meno either unexplainedly acquiesces or is obligingly oblivious.

Socrates examines the hypothesis that "virtue is a good." He remarks that "if there be any sort of good which is distinct from knowledge, virtue may be that good [of course, he has no doubt that knowledge is always a good!]; but if knowledge embraces all good, then we shall be right in thinking that virtue is knowledge." Furthermore, he argues, since "virtue makes us good" (though it is quite likely that there is more than one virtue which "is a good" but does not "make us good") and "all good things are profitable" (surely, "profitable" must be taken in a sense broader than "utilitarian" and not as synonymous with "good"; but in what sense?), it follows that "virtue is profitable." Socrates lists several qualities of body and soul which are profitable, such as beauty and courage, in order to show that they can be harmful unless used wisely. He generalizes that nothing is profitable or hurtful in itself, but everything is "made profitable or hurtful by the addition of wisdom or of folly" (however, even if "folly" is defined as stupidity, folly sometimes results in the profitable; if it is defined as foolishness, it may even be praiseworthy; if it is defined so as to preclude the profitable, then the argument is circular; and if it has some other meaning, what is it?). Since virtue is profitable, Socrates concludes that "virtue is either wholly or partly wisdom"[41] (all that may be correctly deduced, forgetting the previous objections, is that virtue is profitable only when used wisely—and not that virtue "is" in any part wisdom; after all, Socrates does not argue that courage and beauty "are" wisdom, and thus he affords no logical ground to argue that the case is otherwise with regard to virtue; the conclusion is therefore invalid).

Socrates draws the implication that "the good are not by nature good" from the conclusion that virtue is wisdom or knowledge. The implication obviously rests on the assumption that knowledge is acquired and not innate. Socrates adds a second argument, of pragmatic nature, in favor of the implication. He argues that if men were good or virtuous by nature "there would assuredly have been discerners of characters among us who would have known our future great men" and treated them in a special way from their childhood days to be of important service to the state. But, Socrates tacitly contends, history uncovers no such occurrence; therefore men are not virtuous simply by nature. For a similar pragmatic reason, Socrates admits that he also has some doubt about virtue being knowledge. For he still believes that "if virtue is knowledge it may be taught," but "may not the art of which neither teachers nor disciples exist be assumed to be incapable of being taught?" Meno asks him if he really thinks that "there are no teachers of virtue." And Socrates replies: "I have certainly often enquired whether there were any, and taken great pains to find them, and have never succeeded; and many have assisted me in the search, and they were the persons whom I thought the most likely to know."[42]

Twice more it is seen that the pragmatic vein runs deeply in Socrates. It is because no one has been able to forecast reliably who among the young will mature into virtuous men that Socrates questions whether virtue is "natural," and it is because there have been no consistently successful teachers of virtue that he doubts whether virtue is knowledge. Significantly, the latter argument is in opposition to Socrates' first argument which supports the view that the virtuous are not by "nature" virtuous; for that first argument, of logical rather than pragmatic type, concludes that virtue is knowledge. The impression is strong that Socrates favors the pragmatic rather than the logical argument; that he is unsatisfied with the conclusion that virtue is knowledge.

First, the expression of doubt, the pragmatic argument, occurs after the logical argument; this suggests that

Socrates feels some inadequacy in the latter. Second, the logical argument is very weak because of the loopholes (which I have bracketed), and I believe that Socrates is aware of these deficiencies. Third, if exception is taken to my assumption that Socrates is conscious of the weaknesses of his logical argument, the impression that the pragmatic argument takes precedence with Socrates becomes yet stronger. For how can a pragmatic argument cause Socrates to doubt the conclusion of a logically valid argument—the same Socrates who, in the traditional reading of Plato's Dialogues, espouses the supreme reality of the "world" of ideas and the diminished reality of the "world" of senses?! This would place here an even greater weight on the value of pragmatic argument than if he were to know that the logical argument is faulty. Fourth, pragmatic considerations can be sufficiently cogent for Socrates even though they do not carry the stamp of absolute certainty. For the two pragmatic arguments do not have the absolute certainty of a logically valid argument; it is possible that virtue is "natural" even if there have been no reliable discerners of its embryonic stages, and it is possible that virtue is knowledge or teachable even if it has had no successful mentors.

Nevertheless, the pragmatic arguments prevail for Socrates. He is dolorously sensitive to the persistent and pervasive failure to produce virtuous men even with the abiding aid of powerful yearnings and strivings. Until such time as this condition is altered, Socrates cannot believe that virtuous character is adequately predictable or teachable.

The importance of these two pragmatic arguments in Socrates' thought is suggestive of his response to Meno's dilemma about the impossibility of learning. There, too, Socrates embraces only his "second," the pragmatic, solution. Can it be that in general the traditional understanding of Plato's Socrates fails to appreciate sufficiently his concern for the pragmatic? In any case, the pragmatic arguments are primary in the *Meno*; because of them Socrates is somewhat pessimistic and quite nonutopian about the teachability of virtue. The remainder of the *Meno* galvanizes this point.

Anytus, the last of the Dialogue's characters, is now introduced. He is an Athenian politician whose son apparently received a good education, for his son has been chosen to fill high offices of the state. Socrates wants Anytus to point out the successful teachers of virtue, but first Socrates puts a series of questions to him. Is it not true, Socrates asks, that if one wishes to learn how to be a cobbler, physician, or flute-player, one ought to seek out as teachers men who profess these respective arts and who take payment for their instruction? Anytus concurs. Does it not follow, then, Socrates continues, that in order to learn how to be virtuous one ought to go to the Sophists, virtue's professional teachers, for instruction? Anytus vehemently rejects this suggestion: "I only hope that no friend or kinsman or acquaintance of mine, whether citizen or stranger, will ever be so mad as to allow himself to be corrupted by them; for they are a manifest pest and corrupting influence to those who have to do with them." Socrates appears incredulous. "How could that be? A mender of old shoes, or patcher up of clothes, who made the shoes or clothes worse than he received them, could not have remained thirty days undetected, and would very soon have starved; whereas during more than forty years, Protagoras was corrupting all Hellas, and sending his disciples from him worse than he received them [and making a fortune], and he was never found out."[43]

THREE MAJOR HELLENIC CONCEPTIONS OF VIRTUE

The pragmatic argument continues; where are the teachers of virtue? But the main thrust of the above discussion reflects the confrontation of three major Hellenic conceptions of the nature of virtue and its mode of acquisition. Anytus represents the traditional stand. Virtue is to be achieved by the "proper" training of body and mind. The body should be lithe, trim, and strong, but not musclebound, in order to dispatch the "proper" directives of the mind. The "proper" directives to most of life's serious problems are to be found simply and absolutely in the divinely inspired words of the ancient poets—especially in the holy scripture according to Homer. Regular recitation of the Homeric verses produces the "proper" discipline and dogma. Virtuous activity is the train of inspired traditional values.

In the rapidly changing societies of Hellas, it is not surprising that many would find the traditional values and their modes of acquisition uninspired. The Sophists emerged onto the Hellenic scene in order to eradicate the virtue gap. Most of them claimed to eliminate the gap not by the substitution of a new and more adequate conception of the objective nature of virtue, but rather by the banishment of the nature of virtue from the objective orders. Investigation into the rational aspects of the nature of virtue was useless, because what was called "virtue" was merely nonrational conventionality. Moreover, since virtue was merely conventional, it was understandable that moral values differ according to time and place. Virtue is radically subjective, relative, and nonrational; it is not a genuine problem for ethical inquiry.

Once the above metaethical description of virtue is accepted, the clever response is to turn the conventional virtues which are best rewarded by society to one's own advantage—to become proficient in the established values of success. The Sophists claimed to teach such skills by new methods which worked more effectively and quickly than the traditional methods. They professed to teach how to win politico-legal battles and influence people in ten easy lessons in rhetoric and persuasive argumentation. In practice, this was a training in one-upmanship rather than a critique of traditional values of success. Nevertheless, the metaethical and methodological differences brought with them new possibilities, and some of the latter do actualize in changes of value.

Socrates agrees and disagrees (as do Plato and Aristotle) with both the traditionalists and the Sophists. He agrees with the traditionalists that the nature of virtue is located in objective orders, but he does not agree that it can be discovered in the ancient poetical writings without much error, distortion, and incompleteness. Virtuous activity is the healthy, harmonious, and holistic actualization of man's plenteous possibilities. The most satisfactory way of discovering the specific virtues of *homo sapiens* is by the continual scientific investigation of the general aspects of the objective orders of human nature and its condition in the universe. He agrees with the Sophists that no code of morality can be adequate for all times and situations; for the human condition, if not human nature, changes. Thus, he argues in *The Republic,* even the "ideal" state could not prevail perpetually; because "all created things must decay, even a social order of this kind cannot last for ever, but will decline."[44] He even agrees somewhat with the Sophists that to some extent knowledge is deficient in directing ethical activity, for it cannot reliably predict the inevitable chance occurrences, metaphysical drift, or "vagrant alescences."[45] Socrates suggests later in the *Meno* that there are "things which happen by chance [and] are not under the guidance of man."[46] Not only is there constant change in the spatio-temporal order, but the change does not always fit neatly into the contemporary intellectual framework. He undoubtedly would approve of Aristotle's warning that the certainty and precision characteristic of mathematics should not be sought in ethics.[47] Socrates agrees with the Sophists that no rule of morality ought to be interpreted slavishly; that is, without relating it to a sufficiently wide context of the particular problem to which it is to be applied. For example, he indicates in *The Republic* that it would be absurd to return a lethal weapon to a madman because of the dictum that anything borrowed ought to be returned.[48] But, in contradistinction to the Sophists, Socrates would also insist that not all change is ephemeral and no trait is unique in every respect; prevalence and pervasiveness are proceived as well as alescence and insularity.[49] Complexes of uniformities and regularities are encountered which establish the integrities of human nature and condition, and exhibit broad natural obligations and objective standards of health. There is sufficient bed-rock in nature to make human judgment possible, actual, and necessary; to be the ground for a supple naturalistic ethics. It is true, and in many ways tragic, that knowledge of physical nature, human nature, and the nature of society is frequently inadequate for wise judgment; but prudence recommends that the knowledge available be applied hopefully to practical problems and used sanguinely to develop theoretical knowledge. Otherwise, despair will induce paralysis, and the reign of ignorance and tragedy will be guaranteed. Socrates believes this to be true not only with regard to Meno's sophistical dilemma about the impossibility of learning, but also in relation to the Sophists' unwillingness to inquire into the justification of the traditional values of success. He believes that the Sophists are not radical enough, and that they are too quick to legislate normative ethics out of the concern of philosophy. Socrates believes that philosophy can legitimately cope with normative ethics, and have some success with it.

Perhaps it is now more understandable why Socrates does not welcome Anytus as an ally against the Sophists. Anytus is easily excited to inveigh against the Sophists, but he avoids any serious investigation of their position (remember that the historical Anytus is one of the accusers at the historical Socrates' trial). His swooping and sweeping damnations serve to avoid a confrontation with those abuses and deficiencies of traditional values which the Sophists oppose. Socrates agrees with the Sophists that there are shortcomings in the traditional approach, although he differs with the Sophists on the nature of the remedy and probably in the identification of some of the shortcomings. The pragmatic Socrates believes that the persistent popularity of many of the Sophists is strong evidence of insufficiencies in the ancient values, and he is therefore reluctant to ally himself with the establishment. Unlike most men, Socrates is not desperate enough for support to grab onto overt agreement before determining that it contains no significant covert disagreement. The covert disagreement may fester into an inquisition, especially in as unreasoning a man as the next exchange shows Anytus to be.

soc. *Has any of the Sophists wronged you, Anytus? What makes you so angry with them?*
any. *No, indeed, neither I nor any of my belongings has*

*ever had, nor would I suffer them to have, anything to
do with them.*

SOC. *Then you are entirely unacquainted with them?*

ANY. *And I have no wish to be acquainted.*

SOC. *Then, my dear friend, how can you know whether a
thing is good or bad of which you are wholly ignorant?*

ANY. *Quite well; I am sure that I know what manner of
men these are, whether I am acquainted with them
or not.*

SOC. *You must be a diviner, Anytus, for I really cannot make
out, judging from your own words, how, if you are
not acquainted with them, you know about them ....*[50]

S OCRATES ARGUES THAT VIRTUE CANNOT BE TAUGHT

Socrates requests Anytus to recommend a successful
Athenian teacher of virtue. Anytus replies: "Any Athenian
gentleman, taken at random, if he [the student] will mind
him, will do far more good to him than the Sophists." But,
Socrates asks, if these gentlemen's manifestations of virtue
have grown unaided by teaching, how will they be able to
teach virtue? Anytus "imagines" that they learned virtue
from the previous generation of gentlemen—for "have there
not been many good men in this city?" "Certainly," Socrates
responds; "and many good statemen also there always have

been and there are still, in the city of Athens. But the question is whether they were also good teachers of their own virtue;—not whether there are, or have been, good men in this part of the world, but whether virtue can be taught, is the question which we have been discussing." Consider the cases of Themistocles, Aristides, Pericles, and Thucydides, Socrates adds. These were exceptionally wise and virtuous men, but is it not true that their sons were not especially virtuous? Anytus agrees. Surely, Socrates continues, these outstanding gentlemen must have made strenuous efforts to teach their sons virtue, the most valuable art of all; for they succeeded in teaching their sons lesser skills. And yet they failed in teaching their sons virtue. Hence, "once more, I suspect, friend Anytus, that virtue is not a thing which can be taught." Anytus responds, and it is his last speech in the Dialogue.

> ANY. *Socrates, I think that you are too ready to speak evil of men: and, if you will take my advice, I would recommend you to be careful. Perhaps there is no city in which it is not easier to do men harm than to do them good, and this is certainly the case at Athens, as I believe that you know.*
>
> SOC. *O Meno, I think that Anytus is in a rage. And he may well be in a rage, for he thinks, in the first place, that I am defaming these gentlemen; and in the second place, he is of opinion that he is one of them himself. But some day he will know what is the meaning of defamation, and if he ever does, he will forgive me . . . .*[51]

Anytus still reacts irrationally. He does not reply logically to Socrates' argument, but is frightened by the opposition of the conclusion (that virtue is unteachable) to his traditional stand. His "recommendation" to Socrates is a threat, and it sallies from the weakness of his position. His threat and Socrates' reply also reflect Plato's poignant response to the historical confrontation of Anytus and Socrates at Socrates' trial. "But some day he will know what is the meaning of defamation, and if he ever does, he will forgive me." Most important, however, is Socrates' reaffirmation of his pragmatic argument: no consistently successful teacher of virtue can be found, and therefore the great likelihood is that virtue is not completely teachable.

RIGHT OPINION AS A GOOD GUIDE

But then, Meno asks, how do men become virtuous? To answer the question, Socrates draws upon his famous distinction between "knowledge" and "opinion." "Knowledge" signifies a true judgment which is based on adequate evidence or reason; "opinion" signifies a judgment which is based on inadequate evidence or reason; and "right opinion," or "true opinion," signifies a true judgment which is based on inadequate evidence or reason. The previous discussion has been faulty, Socrates says, in claiming that only knowledge is a good guide for action; because right opinion is equally as good a guide. The only excellence which knowledge has and right opinion lacks is stability of good guidance; for right opinion is unrelated to a consideration of evidence, causality, or reason, and is therefore likely to vanish as quickly and illogically as it arises. Nevertheless, while it abides, right opinion is as good a guide as knowledge.

> soc. *And therefore not by any wisdom, and not because*
> *they were wise, did Themistocles and those others of*
> *whom Anytus spoke govern states. This was the reason*
> *why they were unable to make others like themselves—*
> *because their virtue was not grounded on knowledge . . . .*
> *But if not by knowledge, the only alternative which*
> *remains is that statesmen must have guided states by*
> *right opinion, which is in politics what divination is*
> *in religion; for diviners and also prophets say many*
> *things truly, but they know not what they say . . . .*
> *And may we not, Meno, truly call those men 'divine'*
> *who, having no understanding, yet succeed in many a*
> *grand deed and word? . . . Then we shall also be right*
> *in calling divine those whom we were just now speaking*
> *of as diviners and prophets, including the whole tribe*
> *of poets. Yes, and statesmen above all may be said to be*
> *divine and illumined, being inspired and possessed*
> *of God, in which condition they say many grand things,*
> *not knowing what they say . . . . And the women too,*
> *Meno, call good men divine—do they not? and the*
> *Spartans, when they praise a good man, say 'that he is*
> *a divine man.'*

MEN. *And I think, Socrates, that they are right; although very likely our friend Anytus may take offence at the word.*

SOC. *I do not care; as for Anytus, there will be another opportunity of talking with him. To sum up our enquiry—the results seems to be, if we are at all right in our view, that virtue is neither natural nor acquired, but an instinct given by God to the virtuous. Nor is the instinct accompanied by reason, unless there may be supposed to be among statesmen some one who is capable of educating statesmen ....Then, Meno, the conclusion is that virtue comes to the virtuous by the gift of God. But we shall never know the certain truth until, before asking how virtue is given, we enquire into the actual nature of virtue. I fear that I must go away, but do you, now that you are persuaded yourself, persuade our friend Anytus. And do not let him be so exasperated; if you can conciliate him, you will have done good service to the Athenian people.*[52]

THE SIGNIFICANCE OF THE DIALOGUE'S CONCLUSION

And thus does Plato end the *Meno*. He is still deeply pained by his teacher's senseless trial and death. He weaves two references to Anytus into the Dialogue's conclusion primarily because they allude to the historical Socrates' trial. He makes the point that Anytus would probably "take offence" at Socrates' liberal usage of the word "divine." Undoubtedly, Anytus would restrict the word's reference solely to the qualities or actions of the traditional gods, and not extend its reference to any human agency. In fact, one of the charges for which the historical Socrates is tried, as Plato records in his *Apology*, is that of atheism. But Socrates is not fearful; and he shall have "another opportunity" of talking about it with Anytus—at the trial.

The last remark of the Dialogue also alludes to the historical Socrates' trial and conviction. Socrates asks Meno to "conciliate" the "exasperated" Anytus by explaining to Anytus that virtue is considerably unteachable and comes largely by divine dispensation, and if Meno succeeds he "will have done good service to the Athenian people." Plato is convinced that the Athenians have suffered a great loss with the death of Socrates; but if the fear and anger of Anytus and his colleagues had been appeased, the Athenians would have been spared the trial and resultant loss of Socrates.

I believe that there is another level to this last allusion. Plato records in his *Apology* that the historical Socrates is tried on one other charge—that of corrupting the morals of his students. An equivalent way of phrasing this charge would be to say that Socrates was teaching his students to be unvirtuous. But if virtue is to a significant degree unteachable and cannot arise without selective divine dispensation, then there is ground for suspecting that immorality is also considerably unteachable. As a teacher of young men and women, I have no evidence that my teaching has affected my students' morality one way or the other; and I do not think that this result is uncommon among teachers (some teachers may feel this to be deflating, but I find it most comforting). It is especially unlikely that the morality of college-age and adult students can be appreciably altered by the teaching of their professors, parents, or pastors; and Socrates' students were not younger than our college students. Hence, there may be a good pragmatic argument for the conclusion that Socrates could scarcely have corrupted the morality of his students. If Meno could have persuaded Anytus to accept the doctrine of divine dispensation and its consequences, Socrates might not have been brought to trial. But, as Plato draws the characters of Meno and Anytus, such persuasion is unimaginable. Socrates' trial and death are assured; they are the destined dramatic and historic dénouement. Perhaps this mitigates Plato's pain.

Socrates' answer to Meno's persistent question is as follows. The practice of virtue is largely unguided by knowledge; for if knowledge were its guide, then virtue would be teachable and taught. The practice of virtue must be guided then by man's only other right guide—right opinion; "for things which happen by chance are not under the guidance of man." But two questions remain. The first is a refined form of Meno's persistent question; how does the power of practicing virtue, of obtaining right opinions for good guidance, originate? The second is: whence originates that rare power to be quite consistently virtuous, when right opinion is usually a fleeting phenomenon? Socrates' reply to both of these questions is that ultimately these powers are enveloped in mystery, they are chance occurrences. Right opinion, whether evanescent or constant, is a good guide while it prevails; but its genesis is largely beyond human guidance or control. A statesman's consistently good political judgment is more improbable, more mysterious, than political judgment which is only occasionally good; nevertheless, the former does occur. The "many" good deeds and words, the frequent and unwavering true opinions of those few "divine" poets, prophets, and politicians cannot be causally related to "nature" or instruction (acquisition). The same pragmatic arguments which Socrates uses to conclude that "virtue is neither natural nor acquired" when he considers the practice of virtue to arise from knowledge, can be used for the same conclusion now that he understands the practice of virtue to rise from true opinion. If the power to be virtuous is derived from "nature," why are there not any discerners of budding virtue? And if the power to be virtuous is acquired, why are there not any teachers of virtue? Apparently, Socrates does not feel the need to reiterate these arguments.

Socrates' usage of the word "nature," however, requires explanation. I think that by "nature" he intends to signify the regular and knowable order of processes in the universe. But the universe also exhibits powers and events whose sources are not "natural"; whose sources are not located in the order of regular and knowable processes; whose sources are chance happenings or mysteries; nevertheless, whose sources are located in the same universe which embraces "nature." When Socrates says that virtue is not engendered "naturally," I doubt that he wishes to imply that virtue springs from some transcendental "supernatural" force or "world." I prefer to think that he wants to emphasize that the genesis of virtue is not located in the order of "nature," although it is located in the same universe in which "nature" is located. He wants to emphasize that the source of virtue is a mystery, but mystery is not a trait which belongs exclusively to the supernatural. True, Socrates says that virtue is divinely dispensed and an "instinct given by God." But it should be remembered that his definition of "divine" is liberal enough to cover the excellence of human production, while the latter phrase may reflect the theological and psychological biases of the translator's Victorian Christianity. In any case, no matter which of the two interpretations is given to Socrates' denial of "naturalness," the genesis of virtue is, for him, beyond human control; the original differences among individual powers of virtue must be accepted as "given," as brute fact. Nevertheless, Socrates says, there is room and need for more discussion on the nature of virtue, and this is done in later Dialogues.

PUZZLING RECENT APPRAISALS OF PLATO

In view of the *Meno's* open admission of the considerable ignorance surrounding the genesis of virtue, including political virtue, it seems puzzling to find recent critics arguing that Plato is a utopian who wishes the state to adhere rigidly to a "blue-print." In view of the *Meno's* explicit conclusion that the practice of virtue arises primarily from right opinion and not knowledge, it seems equally puzzling to find recent critics arguing that Plato believes that politics can be reduced to an exact science. And this is the Plato who, as an old man, writes in his *Seventh Epistle*:

> *The more I reflected upon what was happening, upon what kind of men were active in politics, and upon the state of our laws and customs, and the older I grew, the more I realized how difficult it is to manage a city's affairs rightly. For I saw it was impossible to do anything without friends and loyal followers; and to find such men ready to hand would be a piece of sheer good luck, since our city was no longer guided by the customs and practices of our fathers, while to train up new ones was anything but easy.*[53]

Some recent critics also see Plato as a totalitarian and an enemy of democracy. Yet Plato, commenting on the totalitarian Rule of Thirty, which included some of his relatives and acquaintances and whose invitation to join them he declined, writes in his *Seventh Epistle:* "But as I watched them they showed in a short time that the preceding [democratic] constitution had been a precious thing....When I saw all this and other like things of no little consequence, I was appalled and drew back from that reign of injustice."[54] And about the democracy which succeeded the Rule of Thirty and convicted Socrates at the trial, Plato writes with unusual understanding: "Now many deplorable things occurred during those troubled days, and it is not surprising that under cover of the revolution too many old enmities were avenged; but in general those who returned from exile acted with great restraint."[55]

How then do these recent critics arrive at their conclusions? I think that they base their views largely on a literal and sometimes not too careful reading of Plato's later Dialogues, and thus they miss the crucial tensionality of his thought which is conveyed by his dramatic approach. A few examples from Plato's later writings will suggest the tensionality which the dramatic method reveals in his political and ethical thought.

PLATO'S DRAMATIC METHOD: VIEWS ON CENSORSHIP

A literal reading of Plato's *Republic* indicates that art would be severely censored and impoverished in the perfect society. Variety in musical mode and rhythm would be prohibited; only uniformity and simplicity would be allowed. Poetical "representation" (dialogue) would be restricted solely to morally good characters, ideas, and events; the portrayal of "bad character, ill-discipline, meanness, or ugliness" in any art form would be forbidden. The purpose of this harsh censorship would be to eliminate the morally corrupting influences of art.[56] But a dramatic approach to Plato's Dialogues would emphasize that his own artistic works violate almost all of these precepts! *The Republic* itself is replete with variety, subtlety, and complexity. *The Republic* itself "represents" forcefully "meanness" and immoral ideas on justice in the statements of Thrasymachus, Glaucon, and Adeimantus. Since his own works belie these austere maxims, I think Plato intends that his remarks on the censorship of art be taken ironically. He seems to be pointing at the absurdity which can result from taking a sound principle and pulling it to an extreme. Surely, some kind and degree of censorship is necessary for the healthy or moral development of the child; but see what happens when a well-meaning but simple-minded utopian makes a crusade of censorship. Art becomes crippled. Yet a vigorous and variegated art is vital to a civilized society. Glaucon's comment on Socrates' "simple life" society would apply here too: "Really, Socrates, you might be catering for a community of pigs!"[57] Plato's point is that his own work exhibits the service to morality which an intelligent violation of the precepts of censorship can accomplish. The important thing is to handle censorship moderately, and not pull it to either extreme.

PLATO'S DRAMATIC METHOD: VIEWS ON SEX

Immediately following the discussion of the role of censorship in the utopian society's education of its Guardians, Plato considers the effects of sexual activity on morality. A literal reading indicates that he censures *any* sexual activity for the Guardians beyond a fatherly kiss. Socrates argues that since self-control and moderation are of the greatest human value, excessive pleasure and excessive pain must be avoided because they go counter to these values. But there is no "greater or keener pleasure than that of sex," and therefore true lovers ought to "have no contact with this sexual pleasure."[58] A dramatic interpretation, however, would come to the opposite conclusion. Here, too, I think that Plato intends to be ironical; here, too, he seems to be pointing to the absurdity which can result from taking a sound principle and pulling it to an extreme. Surely, moderation is often highly valuable, but see what happens when a zealot dogmatizes it. For never to experience intense pleasure and pain is as immoderate as to be addicted to them. Sexual asceticism is as extreme as sexual libertinism. From a perspective narrower than that of his gross proceptive domain, a truly moderate man takes extreme positions and actions on occasion; he discovers new dimensions of experience by an occasional release of his self-control. Otherwise, his life could hardly be called "human." A society which avoids intense pleasures and pains is not even "catering for a community of pigs!" Plato is suggesting that an unthinking literal application of a valuable ideal can convert the ideal into its opposite. The dramatic view of Plato's work seems to be strengthened by the fact that the discussions on censorship and moderation are placed side by side. He seems to be saying that the whole utopian program is almost farcical.

PLATO'S DRAMATIC METHOD: VIEWS ON THE UTOPIAN SOCIETY

Indeed, John Herman Randall, Jr., has brilliantly noted in his famous course on the history of philosophy that at the end of *The Republic,* in the Myth of Er, Plato suggests that the utopian society be taken ironically. According to the myth, a number of souls are given the opportunity to choose the type of future life they prefer. They have a great variety of lives from which to choose, and there are many more good types of life than there are souls; even the soul making the last choice has a variety of good lives remaining from which to select. None of the souls needs to despair; if the choice is wise, the bad lives can be eschewed. All of the souls select on the bases of their experiences in a previous life. The man with the first choice selects hastily and unwisely; he chooses a life of "the greatest tyranny," and it is "his fate to eat his children and suffer other horrors." This man "was one of the souls who had come from heaven, having lived his previous life in a well-governed state, but having owed his goodness to habit and custom and not to knowledge; and indeed, broadly speaking, the greater part of those who came from heaven, being untried by suffering, were caught in this way, while those who came from earth and had suffered themselves and seen others suffer were not so hasty in their choice."[59] I agree with Randall that the "well-governed state" is an allusion to Plato's "perfect" society. Plato seems to be condemning the absurdities of utopianism; again, he is pointing to the inadequacies which are likely to result from taking a sound principle and pulling it to an extreme. Surely, the application of knowledge to the structure and customs of society and to the encouragement of good habits among the citizens may to some extent be done beneficially; but see what happens when a politically potent fanatic adopts science as the means to the millenium.

Life becomes unlivable. The widespread restrictions deci-
mate life's joys. The citizens become incapable of independent thought and action and unable to cope autono-
mously and wisely with novel situations, because most of
the important decisions are made by the few Guardians. And
it does no good to argue that in the perfect society the masses
have no need of independent thought and action; for, apart
from other serious objections, Plato believes, as noted earlier,
that even the ideal state cannot endure forever. The primary
bonds and securities of infancy are inevitably broken, and
humans ought to be helped to live as adults. Therefore, a
good earthly government (and, because of my limited and
paganistic imagination, I cannot fancy it otherwise for a
heavenly government) will greatly encourage its citizens to
self-determination and the taking of wise risks. Plato is rec
ommending that before undertaking drastic reform of society there should be a sufficient apreciation of how much of
the knowable is unknown, and how much is chance and un-
knowable (unpredictable). In placing the Myth of Er at the
end of *The Republic,* Plato seems to be offering its message
as a summary of his views on utopianism.[60]

   In an even later Dialogue, the *Statesman,* Plato
inserts the Myth of Kronos, which also suggest his prefer-
ence of the earthly city with all of its uncertainties and
sufferings above the heavenly city with its guarantees of
welfare. The Stranger tells of a distant past age when the
god Kronos reigns and rigidly controls everything. As in the
Garden of Eden, it is an age when all things come "without

man's labor"; when man has "fruits without stint from trees and bushes [which need] no cultivation but [spring] up spontaneously out of the ground." "Men [rise] up anew into life out of the earth," and for the most part require no clothing. In this era, there are "no political constitutions and no personal possession of wives and children." And as with Isaiah's vision, "savagery [is] nowhere to be found nor preying of creature on creature, nor [does] war rage nor any strife whatsoever." Then this completely regulated reign of Kronos is overthrown; and the dominion of Zeus, who still rules, begins with its attendant toils, tribulations, and hazards. The Stranger asks, "which of these two [reigns] makes for greater happiness?" He replies to his own question:

> The crucial question is—did the nurslings of Kronos make a right use of their time? They had abundance of leisure and the ability to converse with the animals as well as with one another. Did they use all these advantages for philosophical ends? As they associated with one another and with the animals, did they seek to learn from each several tribe of creatures whether its special faculties enabled it to apprehend some distinctive truth not available to the rest which it could bring as its contribution to swell the common treasure store of wisdom? If they really did all this, it is easy to decide that the happiness of the men of that era was a thousandfold greater than ours. But if, when they had taken their fill of eating and of drinking, the discussions they had with each other and with the animals were of the kind that the surviving stories make them out to have been, then, according to my judgment at any rate, it is equally clear what our verdict must be . . . .[61]

Plato seems to be suggesting that the "surviving stories" would be closer to the truth, and that for man a life which encounters risk and challenge is far happier than one in which all needs are assured of satisfaction. In any case, it has been ordained in the reign of Zeus "that the universe must take sole responsibility and control of its course"; so, "by a like ruling, the same impulse bade its constituent elements achieve by their own power, so far as they might, conception, procreation, and rearing of young."[62] In the present age, there can be no doubt but that mighty efforts should be made to achieve self-determination. Plato is also alluding to the community of wives and possessions and the strict regulations on mating which are, according to a literal reading of *The Republic*, recommended for the Guardians of the "ideal" state; he is saying that they are appropriate only under the dispensation of Kronos.

THE TENSION BETWEEN THE RULE OF MEN AND THE RULE OF LAW

Finally, Plato's writing exhibits the tension between the rule of men and the rule of law. "Ideally," Plato indicates in the *Statesman*, the rule of the supremely gifted political artist would be best. Politics has the most comprehensive scope of all the arts, and it would be preferable if the gifted statesman were free to perform his art unfettered by the prescription of law. But the gift of supreme statesmanship is exceedingly rare, and the possibility of its conjunction with a benevolent disposition is infinitesimal. The rule of men is most likely to produce tyranny, which Plato considers as "the most diseased society of all."[63] For these reasons, and others, Plato advocates the rule of law; yet he does not believe it to be a panacea. In *The Republic*, the Guardians are advised not to legislate prodigally; for in a good society laws are largely unnecessary, and in a bad society they are mostly ineffectual.[64] Moreover, there is another serious limitation in law, as the Stranger in the *Statesman* remarks.

> *Law can never issue an injunction binding on all which really embodies what is best for each.... The differences of human personality, the variety of men's activities, and the restless inconstancy of all human affairs make it impossible for any art whatsoever to issue unqualified rules holding good on all questions at all times.... It is impossible, then, for something invariable and unqualified to deal satisfactorily with what is never uniform and constant.*[65]

Nevertheless, under the dominion of Zeus, the rule of wise law is best.

These excursions into Plato's later Dialogues are intended to point at some basic tensions in his thought, the significance of which is either minimized, missed, or misconstrued by some critics. But the excursions are also intended to point up an important incompletion in the *Meno*.

A just reading of the *Meno* could opine that for Plato the practice of virtue is *entirely* unteachable and *entirely* beyond the sway of nature, because the pragmatic arguments conclude without qualification that "virtue is neither natural nor acquired." Yet the excursions show that Plato believes the practice of virtue to be teachable *to some extent,* for he is seen to be deeply concerned with the cultural determinants of virtue; he believes that, *to a degree,* different modes of censorship, sexual customs, opportunities for autonomy, and political sovereignty affect the practice of virtue diversely. I believe that the latter view is truly Plato's and is compatible with the *Meno.* For, although the conclusions of the pragmatic arguments are stated without qualification, the arguments themselves do not logically require such extreme conclusions. It may be pragmatically warranted to conclude that the practice of virtue is *largely* or *considerably* outside nurture's and nature's spheres of influence from the fact that despite great need and effort teachers of virtue and discerners of incipient virtue are nowhere to be found. But there is no compelling reason to conclude that virtue is *entirely* beyond the determinative powers of nurture and nature. It is conceivable that Plato is hinting at this needed qualification when Socrates concludes in his "logical" argument, which immediately precedes the pragmatic arguments, that virtue is "either wholly or partly" wisdom. Moreover, the *Meno* ends on a nontonic note; the sense of incompleteness is there as it is in the beginning and during the course of the Dialogue. In his final speech, Socrates says: "But we shall never know the certain truth [about the divine dispensation of virtue] until, before asking how virtue is given, we enquire into the actual nature of virtue." Socrates and Plato clearly recognize the incompleteness of the discussion, and therefore the later modifications should not be taken as contradictory. This is why in interpreting these segments of the *Meno* I take the liberty of saying that for Socrates the practice of virtue is "largely" or "considerably" outside the scopes of nurture's and nature's influence. Why does not Socrates state these qualifications in the *Meno?* I suppose because he is over-reacting to the excessive optimism of Meno and Anytus, who believe that virtue is easily taught and discerned.

TENSIONALITY IN PLATO'S THOUGHT

There is a strong tendency toward pessimism in Plato's thought, which may more than balance his optimistic inclinations. Perhaps the most fundamental tension in his thought is the pull between ideals and the obstacles to their embodiment. Despite his magnificently original and profound contributions to various orders of knowledge, Plato is anti-utopian about the powers of knowledge. He is sadly aware of the limitations of his knowledge of the learning process; that is part of the main theme of the *Meno*, and it is a refrain heard in other Dialogues. But even today, most psychologists admit that their knowledge of learning is largely lacunal. Plato is unsure of how the forms "inform," or "participate" in, the particulars, and he is puzzled by the mind's capacity to know the Forms. Plato is passionately committed to the ideal of knowledge, but he is dolefully and wisely conscious that the vital ability to produce a virtuous man or statesman is largely beyond the pale of knowledge; that is part of the main theme of his *Republic, Statesman,* and *Meno.* He agonizes about the general fate of worthwhile ideals to be "spoliated"[66] by the precariousness, complexity, and vagrancy in man and the universe; he laments the frequent conversion of these ideals into their opposites by and in the flux and intricacy of actualities. Perhaps Plato even sees the essential incompleteness of all knowledge because he glimpses the shadow of the ultimate and impenetrable mystery of reality: why is any trait of reality (any discriminandum or "natural complex")[67] not otherwise?[68] The tensionality, irony, and moodiness of these thoughts are more movingly and fully conveyed in dramatic than in logical mode.

NOTES

[1] Karl R. Popper, *The Open Society and its Enemies* (revised edition; Princeton: Princeton University Press, 1950), p. 99.

[2] I have learned much about Plato from Woodbridge, Randall, and Buchler of Columbia University, but whatever mistakes there may be in my interpretation I have managed to achieve by myself.

[3] For a profound analysis of these modes of human judgment and of a general metaphysics of human judgment, read Justus Buchler's *Toward a General Theory of Human Judgment* (New York: Columbia University Press, 1951), and *Nature and Judgment* (New York: Columbia University Press, 1955).

[4] This was the description of Plato given by John Herman Randall, Jr., in his course on the history of philosophy.

[5] Buchler, *Toward a General Theory of Human Judgment*, p. 123.

[6] *Ibid.*, p. 124.

[7]Ludwig Wittgenstein, *Tractatus Logico-Philosophicus* (New York: The Humanities Press), p. 3.

[8]Buchler, *Toward a General Theory of Human Judgment,* p. 8.

[9]Plato, *The Republic,* trans. H. D. P. Lee (Baltimore: Penguin Books, 1955), pp. 45-46.

[10]Plato, *Meno,* in *The Dialogues of Plato,* B. Jowett, trans., 3rd ed. (5 vols.; New York: Macmillan and Co., 1892), II, pp. 27-28.

[11]*Ibid.,* p. 28.

[12]*Ibid.,* pp. 28-29.

[13]*Ibid.,* p. 29.

[14]*Ibid.,* p. 30.

[15]*Ibid.,* pp. 30-31.

[16]*Ibid.,* p. 31.

[17]*Ibid.,* pp. 32-33.

[18]*Ibid.,* p. 33. The emphasis is mine.

[19]In the opening segments of *The Republic,* Plato again reveals dramatically the tendency of Socrates to respond appositionally to the tenor of his partner's discourse. Cephalus is friendly, intelligent, moderate; Socrates treats him respectfully, perhaps even affectionately. Polemarchus is dogmatic and stupid in his discussion of the nature of justice and Socrates dismisses him with absurd arguments. Thrasymachus delivers his views on justice more intelligently, yet in a very antagonistic manner toward Socrates. Some of Socrates' counterarguments are sound and some are not, but Socrates is extremely sarcastic toward him. Glaucon recognizes the logical inadequacies of Socrates' responses and says to Socrates (p. 89): "For you seem to have fascinated Thrasymachus into a premature submission, like a snake-charmer; but I am not satisfied yet about justice and injustice." Surely, Plato does not accept all of Socrates' statements.

[20]*Ibid.,* p. 35.

[21]*Ibid.,* p. 38.

[22]*Ibid.,* p. 39.

[23]*Ibid.,* pp. 39-40.

[24]*Ibid.,* pp. 40-41.

[25]The history of ideas reveals the great difficulty which philosophers have in altering their basic categories even when such categories lead to dead-ends. For example, Bertrand Russell conceives experience to be private and atomistic, and then is forced to regard interpersonal communication as miraculous —even though the uncountable frequency of interpersonal communication dispels any hint of miraculousness. Apparently, Russell finds it hard to change to a social and contextual view of experience, as Pragmatists and others do; although, among other benefits, interpersonal communication would then be taken as a completely natural phenomenon.

[26]Plato, *Meno,* p. 41.

[27]It will not do to argue that Socrates takes "prove" as synonymous with "recollect"; for why would he then not also take "teach" as synonymous with "recollect?"

[28]Plato, *Meno,* p. 42.

[29]*Ibid.,* p. 45.

[30]*Ibid.,* p. 47.

[31]*Ibid.*

[32]*Ibid.,* p. 43.

[33]*Ibid.,* p. 45.

[34]*Ibid.,* p. 44.

[35]*Ibid.,* pp. 44-45.

[36]*Ibid.,* p. 39.

[37]*Ibid.,* pp. 46-47.

[38]*Ibid.,* p. 48.

[39]*Ibid.,* p. 47.

[40]*Ibid.,* pp. 48-49.

[41]*Ibid.,* pp. 49-50.

[42]*Ibid.,* p. 51.

[43]*Ibid.,* p. 53.

[44]Plato, *The Republic,* p. 315.

[45]J. Buchler, *Metaphysics of Natural Complexes* (New York: Columbia University Press, 1966), pp. 57, 60, 65, 66.

[46]Plato, *Meno,* p. 62.

[47]Richard McKeon (ed.), *The Basic Works of Aristole* (New York: Random House, 1941), p. 936.

[48]Plato, *The Republic,* p. 55.
[49]Buchler, *Metaphysics of Natural Complexes,* pp. 52-92.
[50]Plato, *Meno,* p. 54.
[51]*Ibid.,* pp. 54-57.
[52]*Ibid.,* pp. 62-63.
[53]Plato, *Epistles,* trans. Glenn R. Morrow (Indianapolis: Bobbs-Merrill Co., Inc., Library of Liberal Arts, 1962), p. 217.
[54]*Ibid.,* p. 216.
[55]*Ibid.* Recently, doubt has been cast upon the authenticity of the Seventh Epistle.
[56]Plato, *The Republic,* pp. 126-142.
[57]*Ibid.,* p. 106.
[58]*Ibid.,* p. 144.
[59]*Ibid.,* p. 399.
[60]After this essay was written, Randall's article, "Plato on the Good Life and Spartan Ideal," appeared in the *Journal of the History of Ideas,* XXVIII (July-September, 1967), 307-324. He puts into print there his interpretation of the Myth of Er (pp. 318-319), as well as some other implications of taking Plato seriously as "the artist-philosopher." My great debt to his lectures becomes obvious.

There are some assertions in the article, however, to which I take exception. I differ with the following part of Randall's view of Plato's philosophy of education (p. 316).

> ... Plato rejects also any education in the "social studies"; that is all "mere opinion." There is no evidence that "good citizenship"... can possibly be taught....
> It is significant that Plato does not stand for teaching the "social sciences": he was convinced there is no such thing....

But in the next-to-last paragraph, I argue that for Plato the practice of virtue, which includes "good citizenship," is not *entirely* unteachable, and that it is *to some extent* determined by cultural conditions. It is difficult for me to believe that Plato denies utterly the actuality and possibility of the "social sciences." How, then, can we account for his amazing anticipations of profound psychological, sociological, and political insights; for the educational goal of his Academy as "a training-ground for rulers, not only maintaining a particular political theory, but also furnishing practical guidance to such of its members who had attained to political power" (Wormell, *Literary Tradition Concerning Hermius of Atarneus*, as quoted by Lee in Plato's *The Republic*: Penguin Books, p. 17); and for the considerable amount of time, trouble, and danger involved in his attempt to educate Dionysius II at Syracuse as a philosophic statesman? True, the latter two "facts" have not been adequately established.

I also disagree with Randall in that he, following his teacher, Woodbridge (*Son of Apollo*), understands the "demonstration" with Meno's slave as suggesting that "you can teach even an ignorant slave-boy the truths of geometry, for they are not debatable, while the wisest of men cannot teach their own sons moral excellence" (p. 315). In my view, the "demonstration" is a farce; it is not at all an example of teaching. I agree with Randall and Woodbridge that Plato considers the study of geometry to be an excellent preparation for attaining an objective attitude, but I think that one must find in Plato sources other than the slave-boy "demonstration" to support this contention.

[61]Plato, *Statesman*, trans. J. B. Skemp, ed. Martin Ostwald (Indianapolis: Bobbs-Merrill Co., Inc., Liberal Arts Press, Inc., 1957), pp. 28-29.
[62]*Ibid.*, p. 31.
[63]Plato, *The Republic*, p. 313.
[64]*Ibid.*, pp. 170-173.
[65]Plato, *Statesman*, p. 66.
[66]Buchler, *Metaphysics of Natural Complexes*, pp. 57, 60, 61, 64.
[67]*Ibid.*, pp. 1-3.
[68]*Ibid.*, pp. 97-99.

MENO

PERSONS OF
THE DIALOGUE ⟪
MENO ⟪ SOCRATES
⟪ A SLAVE OF MENO
⟪ ANYTUS

Meno. CAN you tell me, Socrates, whether virtue is acquired by teaching or by practice; or if neither by teaching nor by practice, then whether it comes to man by nature, or in what other way?

Socrates. O Meno, there was a time when the Thessalians were famous among the other Hellenes only for their riches and their riding; but now, if I am not mistaken, they are equally famous for their wisdom, especially at Larisa, which is the native city of your friend Aristippus. And this is Gorgias' doing; for when he came there, the flower of the Aleuadae, among them your admirer Aristippus, and the other chiefs of the Thessalians, fell in love with his wisdom. And he has taught you the habit of answering questions in a grand and bold style, which becomes those who know, and is the style in which he himself answers all comers; and any Hellene who likes may ask him anything. How different is our lot! my dear Meno. Here at Athens there is a dearth of the commodity, and all wisdom seems to have emigrated from us to you. I am certain that if you were to ask any Athenian whether virtue was natural or acquired, he would laugh in your face, and say: 'Stranger, you have far too good an opinion of me, if you think that I can answer your question. For I literally do not know what virtue is, and much less whether it is acquired by teaching or not.' And I myself, Meno, living as I do in this region of poverty, am as poor as the rest of the world; and I confess with shame that I know literally nothing about virtue; and when I do not know the 'quid' of anything how can I know the 'quale'? How, if I knew nothing at all of Meno, could I tell if he was fair, or the opposite of fair; rich and noble, or the reverse of rich and noble? Do you think that I could?

Men. No, indeed. But are you in earnest, Socrates, in saying that you do not know what virtue is? And am I to carry back this report of you to Thessaly?

Soc. Not only that, my dear boy, but you may say further that I have never known of any one else who did, in my judgment.

Men. Then you have never met Gorgias when he was at Athens?

Soc. Yes, I have.

Men. And did you not think that he knew?

Soc. I have not a good memory, Meno, and therefore I cannot now tell what I thought of him at the time. And I dare say that he did know, and that you know what he said: please, therefore, to remind me of what he said; or, if you would rather, tell me your own view; for I suspect that you and he think much alike.

Men. Very true.

Soc. Then as he is not here, never mind him, and do you tell me: By the gods, Meno, be generous, and tell me what you say that virtue is; for I shall be truly delighted to find that I have been mistaken, and that you and Gorgias do really have this knowledge; although I have been just saying that I have never found anybody who had.

Men. There will be no difficulty, Socrates, in answering your question. Let us take first the virtue of a man — he should know how to administer the state, and in the administration of it to benefit his friends and harm his enemies; and he must also be careful not to suffer harm himself. A woman's virtue, if you wish to know about that, may also be easily described: her duty is to order her house, and keep what is indoors, and obey her husband. Every age, every condition of life, young or old, male or female, bond or free, has a different virtue: there are virtues numberless, and no lack of definitions of them; for virtue is relative to the actions and ages of each of us in all that we do. And the same may be said of vice, Socrates [1].

Soc. How fortunate I am, Meno! When I ask you for one virtue, you present me with a swarm of them [2], which are in your keeping. Suppose that I carry on the figure of the swarm, and ask of you, What is the nature of the bee? and you answer that there are many kinds of bees, and I reply: But do bees differ as bees, because there are many and different kinds of them; or are they not rather to be distinguished by some other quality, as for example beauty, size, or shape? How would you answer me?

Men. I should answer that bees do not differ from one another, as bees.

Soc. And if I went on to say: That is what I desire to know, Meno; tell me what is the quality in which they do not differ, but are all alike;— would you be able to answer?

Men. I should.

Soc. And so of the virtues, however many and different they may be, they have all a common nature which makes them virtues; and on this he who would answer the question, 'What is virtue?' would do well to have his eye fixed: Do you understand?

Men. I am beginning to understand; but I do not as yet take hold of the question as I could wish.

Soc. When you say, Meno, that there is one virtue of a man, another of a woman, another of a child, and so on, does this apply only to virtue, or would you say the same of health, and size, and strength? Or is the nature of health always the same, whether in man or woman?

Men. I should say that health is the same, both in man and woman.

Soc. And is not this true of size and strength? If a woman is strong, she will be strong by reason of the same form and of the same strength subsisting in her which there is in the man. I mean to say that strength, as strength, whether of man or woman, is the same. Is there any difference?

---

[1] Cp. Arist. Pol. i. 13, § 10.   [2] Cp. Theaet. 146 D.

Men. I think not.

Soc. And will not virtue, as virtue, be the same, whether in a child or in a grown-up person, in a woman or in a man?

Men. I cannot help feeling, Socrates, that this case is different from the others.

Soc. But why? Were you not saying that the virtue of a man was to order a state, and the virtue of a woman was to order a house?

Men. I did say so.

Soc. And can either house or state or anything be well ordered without temperance and without justice?

Men. Certainly not.

Soc. Then they who order a state or a house temperately or justly order them with temperance and justice?

Men. Certainly.

Soc. Then both men and women, if they are to be good men and women, must have the same virtues of temperance and justice?

Men. True.

Soc. And can either a young man or an elder one be good, if they are intemperate and unjust?

Men. They cannot.

Soc. They must be temperate and just?

Men. Yes.

Soc. Then all men are good in the same way, and by participation in the same virtues?

Men. Such is the inference.

Soc. And they surely would not have been good in the same way, unless their virtue had been the same?

Men. They would not.

Soc. Then now that the sameness of all virtue has been proven, try and remember what you and Gorgias say that virtue is.

Men. Will you have one definition of them all?

Soc. That is what I am seeking.

Men. If you want to have one definition of them all, I know not what to say, but that virtue is the power of governing mankind.

Soc. And does this definition of virtue include all virtue?

Is virtue the same in a child and in a slave, Meno? Can the child govern his father, or the slave his master; and would he who governed be any longer a slave?

Men. I think not, Socrates.

Soc. No, indeed; there would be small reason in that. Yet once more, fair friend; according to you, virtue is 'the power of governing;' but do you not add 'justly and not unjustly'?

Men. Yes, Socrates; I agree there; for justice is virtue.

Soc. Would you say 'virtue,' Meno, or 'a virtue'?

Men. What do you mean?

Soc. I mean as I might say about anything; that a round, for example, is 'a figure' and not simply 'figure,' and I should adopt this mode of speaking, because there are other figures.

Men. Quite right; and that is just what I am saying about virtue — that there are other virtues as well as justice.

Soc. What are they? tell me the names of them, as I would tell you the names of the other figures if you asked me.

Men. Courage and temperance and wisdom and magnanimity are virtues; and there are many others.

Soc. Yes, Meno; and again we are in the same case: in searching after one virtue we have found many, though not in the same way as before; but we have been unable to find the common virtue which runs through them all.

Men. Why, Socrates, even now I am not able to follow you in the attempt to get at one common notion of virtue as of other things.

Soc. No wonder; but I will try to get nearer if I can, for you know that all things have a common notion. Suppose now that some one asked you the question which I asked before: Meno, he would say, what is figure? And if you answered 'roundness,' he would reply to you, in my way of speaking, by asking whether you would say that roundness is 'figure' or 'a figure;' and you would answer 'a figure.'

Men. Certainly.

Soc. And for this reason — that there are other figures?

Men. Yes.

Soc. And if he proceeded to ask, What other figures are there? you would have told him.

Men. I should.

Soc. And if he similarly asked what colour is, and you answered whiteness, and the questioner rejoined, Would you say that whiteness is colour or a colour? you would reply, A colour, because there are other colours as well.

Men. I should.

Soc. And if he had said, Tell me what they are?— you would have told him of other colours which are colours just as much as whiteness.

Men. Yes.

Soc. And suppose that he were to pursue the matter in my way, he would say: Ever and anon we are landed in particulars, but this is not what I want; tell me then, since you call them by a common name, and say that they are all figures, even when opposed to one another, what is that common nature which you designate as figure — which contains straight as well as round, and is no more one than the other — that would be your mode of speaking?

Men. Yes.

Soc. And in speaking thus, you do not mean to say that the round is round any more than straight, or the straight any more straight than round?

Men. Certainly not.

Soc. You only assert that the round figure is not more a figure than the straight, or the straight than the round?

Men. Very true.

Soc. To what then do we give the name of figure? Try and answer. Suppose that when a person asked you this question either about figure or colour, you were to reply, Man, I do not understand what you want, or know what you are saying; he would look rather astonished and say: Do you not understand that I am looking for the 'simile in multis'? And then he might put the question in another form: Meno, he might say, what is that 'simile in multis' which you call figure, and which includes not only round and straight figures, but all? Could you not answer that question, Meno? I wish that you would try; the attempt will be good practice with a view to the answer about virtue.

Men. I would rather that you should answer, Socrates.

Soc. Shall I indulge you?

Men. By all means.

Soc. And then you will tell me about virtue?

Men. I will.

Soc. Then I must do my best, for there is a prize to be won.

Men. Certainly.

Soc. Well, I will try and explain to you what figure is. What do you say to this answer?— Figure is the only thing which always follows colour. Will you be satisfied with it, as I am sure that I should be, if you would let me have a similar definition of virtue?

Men. But, Socrates, it is such a simple answer.

Soc. Why simple?

Men. Because, according to you, figure is that which always follows colour.

(*Soc.* Granted).

Men. But if a person were to say that he does not know what colour is, any more than what figure is — what sort of answer would you have given him?

Soc. I 'should have told him the truth. And if he were a philosopher of the eristic and antagonistic sort, I should say to him: You have my answer, and if I am wrong, your business is to take up the argument and refute me. But if we were friends, and were talking as you and I are now, I should reply in a milder strain and more in the dialectician's vein; that is to say, I should not only speak the truth, but I should make use of premisses which the person interrogated would be willing to admit. And this is the way in which I shall endeavour to approach you. You will acknowledge, will you not, that there is such a thing as an end, or termination, or extremity?— all which words I use in the same sense, although I am aware that Prodicus might draw distinctions about them: but still you, I am sure, would speak of a thing as ended or terminated — that is all which I am saying — not anything very difficult.

Men. Yes, I should; and I believe that I understand your meaning.

Soc. And you would speak of a surface and also of a solid, as for example in geometry.

Men. Yes.

Soc. Well then, you are now in a condition to understand

my definition of figure. I define figure to be that in which the solid ends; or, more concisely, the limit of solid.

Men. And now, Socrates, what is colour?

Soc. You are outrageous, Meno, in thus plaguing a poor old man to give you an answer, when you will not take the trouble of remembering what is Gorgias' definition of virtue.

Men. When you have told me what I ask, I will tell you, Socrates.

Soc. A man who was blindfolded has only to hear you talking, and he would know that you are a fair creature and have still many lovers.

Men. Why do you think so?

Soc. Why, because you always speak in imperatives: like all beauties when they are in their prime, you are tyrannical; and also, as I suspect, you have found out that I have a weakness for the fair, and therefore to humour you I must answer.

Men. Please do.

Soc. Would you like me to answer you after the manner of Gorgias, which is familiar to you?

Men. I should like nothing better.

Soc. Do not he and you and Empedocles say that there are certain effluences of existence?

Men. Certainly.

Soc. And passages into which and through which the effluences pass?

Men. Exactly.

Soc. And some of the effluences fit into the passages, and some of them are too small or too large?

Men. True.

Soc. And there is such a thing as sight?

Men. Yes.

Soc. And now, as Pindar says, 'read my meaning: '— colour is an effluence of form, commensurate with sight, and palpable to sense.

Men. That, Socrates, appears to me to be an admirable answer.

Soc. Why, yes, because it happens to be one which you have been in the habit of hearing: and your wit will have discovered, I suspect, that you may explain in the same way the nature of sound and smell, and of many other similar phenomena.

Men. Quite true.

Soc. The answer, Meno, was in the orthodox solemn vein, and therefore was more acceptable to you than the other answer about figure.

Men. Yes.

Soc. And yet, O son of Alexidemus, I cannot help thinking that the other was the better; and I am sure that you would be of the same opinion, if you would only stay and be initiated, and were not compelled, as you said yesterday, to go away before the mysteries.

Men. But I will stay, Socrates, if you will give me many such answers.

Soc. Well then, for my own sake as well as for yours, I will do my very best; but I am afraid that I shall not be able to give you very many as good: and now, in your turn, you are to fulfil your promise, and tell me what virtue is in the universal; and do not make a singular into a plural, as the facetious say of those who break a thing, but deliver virtue to me whole and sound, and not broken into a number of pieces: I have given you the pattern.

Men. Well then, Socrates, virtue, as I take it, is when he, who desires the honourable, is able to provide it for himself; so the poet says, and I say too —

' Virtue is the desire of things honourable and the power of attaining them.'

Soc. And does he who desires the honourable also desire the good?

Men. Certainly.

Soc. Then are there some who desire the evil and others who desire the good? Do not all men, my dear sir, desire good?

Men. I think not.

Soc. There are some who desire evil?

Men. Yes.

Soc. Do you mean that they think the evils which they desire, to be good; or do they know that they are evil and yet desire them?

Men. Both, I think.

Soc. And do you really imagine, Meno, that a man **knows** evils to be evils and desires them notwithstanding?

Men. Certainly I do.

Soc. And desire is of possession?

Men. Yes, of possession.

Soc. And does he think that the evils will do good to him who possesses them, or does he know that they will do him harm?

Men. There are some who think that the evils will do them good, and others who know that they will do them harm.

Soc. And, in your opinion, do those who think that they will do them good know that they are evils?

Men. Certainly not.

Soc. Is it not obvious that those who are ignorant of their nature do not desire them; but they desire what they suppose to be goods although they are really evils; and if they are mistaken and suppose the evils to be goods they really desire goods?

Men. Yes, in that case.

Soc. Well, and do those who, as you say, desire evils, and think that evils are hurtful to the possessor of them, know that they will be hurt by them?

Men. They must know it.

Soc. And must they not suppose that those who are hurt are miserable in proportion to the hurt which is inflicted upon them?

Men. How can it be otherwise?

Soc. But are not the miserable ill-fated?

Men. Yes, indeed.

Soc. And does any one desire to be miserable and ill-fated?

Men. I should say not, Socrates.

Soc. But if there is no one who desires to be miserable, there is no one, Meno, who desires evil; for what is misery but the desire and possession of evil?

Men. That appears to be the truth, Socrates, and I admit that nobody desires evil.

Soc. And yet, were you not saying just now that virtue is the desire and power of attaining good?

Men. Yes, I did say so.

Soc. But if this be affirmed, then the desire of good is common to all, and one man is no better than another in that respect?

Men. True.

Soc. And if one man is not better than another in desiring good, he must be better in the power of attaining it?

Men. Exactly.

Soc. Then, according to your definition, virtue would appear to be the power of attaining good?

Men. I entirely approve, Socrates, of the manner in which you now view this matter.

Soc. Then let us see whether what you say is true from another point of view; for very likely you may be right:— You affirm virtue to be the power of attaining goods?

Men. Yes.

Soc. And the goods which you mean are such as health and wealth and the possession of gold and silver, and having office and honour in the state — those are what you would call goods?

Men. Yes, I should include all those.

Soc. Then, according to Meno, who is the hereditary friend of the great king, virtue is the power of getting silver and gold; and would you add that they must be gained piously, justly, or do you deem this to be of no consequence? And is any mode of acquisition, even if unjust or dishonest, equally to be deemed virtue?

Men. Not virtue, Socrates, but vice.

Soc. Then justice or temperance or holiness, or some other part of virtue, as would appear, must accompany the acquisition, and without them the mere acquisition of good will not be virtue.

Men. Why, how can there be virtue without these?

Soc. And the non-acquisition of gold and silver in a dishonest manner for oneself or another, or in other words the want of them, may be equally virtue?

Men. True.

Soc. Then the acquisition of such goods is no more virtue than the non-acquisition and want of them, but whatever is accompanied by justice or honesty is virtue, and whatever is devoid of justice is vice.

Men. It cannot be otherwise, in my judgment.

Soc. And were we not saying just now that justice, temperance, and the like, were each of them a part of virtue?

Men. Yes.

Soc. And so, Meno, this is the way in which you mock me.

Men. Why do you say that, Socrates?

Soc. Why, because I asked you to deliver virtue into my hands whole and unbroken, and I gave you a pattern according to which you were to frame your answer; and you have forgotten already, and tell me that virtue is the power of attaining good justly, or with justice; and justice you acknowledge to be a part of virtue.

Men. Yes.

Soc. Then it follows from your own admissions, that virtue is doing what you do with a part of virtue; for justice and the like are said by you to be parts of virtue.

Men. What of that?

Soc. What of that! Why, did not I ask you to tell me the nature of virtue as a whole? And you are very far from telling me this; but declare every action to be virtue which is done with a part of virtue; as though you had told me and I must already know the whole of virtue, and this too when frittered away into little pieces. And, therefore, my dear Meno, I fear that I must begin again and repeat the same question: What is virtue? for otherwise, I can only say, that every action done with a part of virtue is virtue; what else is the meaning of saying that every action done with justice is virtue? Ought I not to ask the question over again; for can any one who does not know virtue know a part of virtue?

Men. No; I do not say that he can.

Soc. Do you remember how, in the example of figure, we rejected any answer given in terms which were as yet unexplained or unadmitted?

Men. Yes, Socrates; and we were quite right in doing so.

Soc. But then, my friend, do not suppose that we can explain to any one the nature of virtue as a whole through some unexplained portion of virtue, or anything at all in that fashion; we should only have to ask over again the old question, What is virtue? Am I not right?

Men. I believe that you are.

Soc. Then begin again, and answer me, What, according to you and your friend Gorgias, is the definition of virtue?

Men. O Socrates, I used to be told, before I knew you, that you were always doubting yourself and making others doubt; and now you are casting your spells over me, and I am simply getting bewitched and enchanted, and am at my wits' end. And if I may venture to make a jest upon you, you seem to me both in your appearance and in your power over others to be very like the flat torpedo fish, who torpifies those who come near him and touch him, as you have now torpified me, I think. For my soul and my tongue are really torpid, and I do not know how to answer you; and though I have been delivered of an infinite variety of speeches about virtue before now, and to many persons — and very good ones they were, as I thought — at this moment I cannot even say what virtue is. And I think that you are very wise in not voyaging and going away from home, for if you did in other places as you do in Athens, you would be cast into prison as a magician.

Soc. You are a rogue, Meno, and had all but caught me.

Men. What do you mean, Socrates?

Soc. I can tell why you made a simile about me.

Men. Why?

Soc. In order that I might make another simile about you. For I know that all pretty young gentlemen like to have pretty similes made about them — as well they may — but I shall not return the compliment. As to my being a torpedo, if the torpedo is torpid as well as the cause of torpidity in others, then indeed I am a torpedo, but not otherwise; for I perplex others, not because I am clear, but because I am utterly perplexed myself. And now I know not what virtue is, and you seem to be in the same case, although you did once perhaps know before you touched me. However, I have no objection to join with you in the enquiry.

Men. And how will you enquire, Socrates, into that which you do not know? What will you put forth as the subject of enquiry? And if you find what you want, how will you ever know that this is the thing which you did not know?

Soc. I know, Meno, what you mean; but just see what a tiresome dispute you are introducing. You argue that a man cannot enquire either about that which he knows, or about that which he does not know; for if he knows, he has no need to enquire; and if not, he cannot; for he does not know the very subject about which he is to enquire [1].

Men. Well, Socrates, and is not the argument sound?

Soc. I think not.

Men. Why not?

Soc. I will tell you why: I have heard from certain wise men and women who spoke of things divine that —

Men. What did they say?

Soc. They spoke of a glorious truth, as I conceive.

Men. What was it? and who were they?

Soc. Some of them were priests and priestesses, who had studied how they might be able to give a reason of their profession: there have been poets also, who spoke of these things by inspiration, like Pindar, and many others who were inspired. And they say — mark, now, and see whether their words are true — they say that the soul of man is immortal, and at one time has an end, which is termed dying, and at another time is born again, but is never destroyed. And the moral is, that a man ought to live always in perfect holiness. '*For in the ninth year Persephone sends the souls of those from whom she has received the penalty of ancient crime back again from beneath into the light of the sun above, and these are they who become noble kings and mighty men and great in wisdom and are called saintly heroes in after ages* [2].' The soul, then, as being immortal, and having been born again many times, and having seen all things that exist, whether in this world or in the world below, has knowledge of them all; and it is no wonder that she should be able to call to remembrance all that she ever knew about virtue, and about everything; for as all nature is akin, and the soul has learned all things, there is no difficulty in her eliciting or as men say learning, out of a single recollection all the rest, if a man is strenuous and does not faint; for all enquiry and all learning is but recollection. And therefore we ought not to listen to this sophistical argument about the impossibility of enquiry: for it will make us idle, and is sweet only to the

[1] Cp. Aristot. Post. Anal. I. i. 6.   [2] Pindar, Frag. 98 (Boeckh).

sluggard; but the other saying will make us active and inquisitive. In that confiding, I will gladly enquire with you into the nature of virtue.

Men. Yes, Socrates; but what do you mean by saying that we do not learn, and that what we call learning is only a process of recollection? Can you teach me how this is?

Soc. I told you, Meno, just now that you were a rogue, and now you ask whether I can teach you, when I am saying that there is no teaching, but only recollection; and thus you imagine that you will involve me in a contradiction.

Men. Indeed, Socrates, I protest that I had no such intention. I only asked the question from habit; but if you can prove to me that what you say is true, I wish that you would.

Soc. It will be no easy matter, but I will try to please you to the utmost of my power. Suppose that you call one of your numerous attendants, that I may demonstrate on him.

Men. Certainly. Come hither, boy.

Soc. He is Greek, and speaks Greek, does he not?

Men. Yes, indeed; he was born in the house.

Soc. Attend now to the questions which I ask him, and observe whether he learns of me or only remembers.

Men. I will.

Soc. Tell me, boy, do you know that a figure like this is a square?

Boy. I do.

Soc. And you know that a square figure has these four lines equal?

Boy. Certainly.

Soc. And these lines which I have drawn through the middle of the square are also equal?

Boy. Yes.

Soc. A square may be of any size?

Boy. Certainly.

Soc. And if one side of the figure be of two feet, and the other side be of two feet, how much will the whole be? Let me explain: if in one direction the space was of two feet, and in the other direction of one foot, the whole would be of two feet taken once?

Boy. Yes.

Soc. But since this side is also of two feet, there are twice two feet?

Boy. There are.

Soc. Then the square is of twice two feet?

Boy. Yes.

Soc. And how many are twice two feet? count and tell me.

Boy. Four, Socrates.

Soc. And might there not be another square twice as large as this, and having like this the lines equal?

Boy. Yes.

Soc. And of how many feet will that be?

Boy. Of eight feet.

Soc. And now try and tell me the length of the line which forms the side of that double square: this is two feet — what will that be?

Boy. Clearly, Socrates, it will be double.

Soc. Do you observe, Meno, that I am not teaching the boy anything, but only asking him questions; and now he fancies that he knows how long a line is necessary in order to produce a figure of eight square feet; does he not?

Men. Yes.

Soc. And does he really know?

Men. Certainly not.

Soc. He only guesses that because the square is double, the line is double.

Men. True.

Soc. Observe him while he recalls the steps in regular order. (*To the Boy.*) Tell me, boy, do you assert that a double space comes from a double line? Remember that I am not speaking of an oblong, but of a figure equal every way, and twice the size of this — that is to say of eight feet; and I want to know whether you still say that a double square comes from a double line?

Boy. Yes.

Soc. But does not this line become doubled if we add another such line here?

Boy. Certainly.

Soc. And four such lines will make a space containing eight feet?

Boy. Yes.

Soc. Let us describe such a figure: Would you not say that this is the figure of eight feet?

Boy. Yes.

Soc. And are there not these four divisions in the figure, each of which is equal to the figure of four feet?

Boy. True.

Soc. And is not that four times four?

Boy. Certainly.

Soc. And four times is not double?

Boy. No, indeed.

Soc. But how much?

Boy. Four times as much.

Soc. Therefore the double line, boy, has given a space, not twice, but four times as much.

Boy. True.

Soc. Four times four are sixteen — are they not?

Boy. Yes.

Soc. What line would give you a space of eight feet, as this gives one of sixteen feet; — do you see?

Boy. Yes.

Soc. And the space of four feet is made from this half line?

Boy. Yes.

Soc. Good; and is not a space of eight feet twice the size of this, and half the size of the other?

Boy. Certainly.

Soc. Such a space, then, will be made out of a line greater than this one, and less than that one?

Boy. Yes; I think so.

Soc. Very good; I like to hear you say what you think. And now tell me, is not this a line of two feet and that of four?

Boy. Yes.

Soc. Then the line which forms the side of eight feet ought to be more than this line of two feet, and less than the other of four feet?

Boy. It ought.

Soc. Try and see if you can tell me how much it will be.

Boy. Three feet.

Soc. Then if we add a half to this line of two, that will be the line of three. Here are two and there is one; and on the other side, here are two also and there is one: and that makes the figure of which you speak?

Boy. Yes.

Soc. But if there are three feet this way and three feet that way, the whole space will be three times three feet?

Boy. That is evident.

Soc. And how much are three times three feet?

Boy. Nine.

Soc. And how much is the double of four?

Boy. Eight.

Soc. Then the figure of eight is not made out of a line of three?

Boy. No.

Soc. But from what line? — tell me exactly; and if you would rather not reckon, try and show me the line.

Boy. Indeed, Socrates, I do not know.

Soc. Do you see, Meno, what advances he has made in his power of recollection? He did not know at first, and he does not know now, what is the side of a figure of eight feet: but then he thought that he knew, and answered confidently as if he knew, and had no difficulty; now he has a difficulty, and neither knows nor fancies that he knows.

Men. True.

Soc. Is he not better off in knowing his ignorance?

Men. I think that he is.

Soc. If we have made him doubt, and given him the 'torpedo's shock,' have we done him any harm?

Men. I think not.

Soc. We have certainly, as would seem, assisted him in some degree to the discovery of the truth; and now he will wish to remedy his ignorance, but then he would have been ready to tell all the world again and again that the double space should have a double side.

Men. True.

Soc. But do you suppose that he would ever have enquired into or learned what he fancied that he knew, though he was really ignorant of it, until he had fallen into perplexity under the idea that he did not know, and had desired to know?

Men. I think not, Socrates.

Soc. Then he was the better for the torpedo's touch?

Men. I think so.

Soc. Mark now the farther development. I shall only ask him, and not teach him, and he shall share the enquiry with me: and do you watch and see if you find me telling or explaining anything to him, instead of eliciting his opinion. Tell me, boy, is not this a square of four feet which I have drawn?

Boy. Yes.

Soc. And now I add another square equal to the former one?

Boy. Yes.

Soc. And a third, which is equal to either of them?

Boy. Yes.

Soc. Suppose that we fill up the vacant corner?

Boy. Very good.

Soc. Here, then, there are four equal spaces?

Boy. Yes.

Soc. And how many times larger is this space than this other?

Boy. Four times.

Soc. But it ought to have been twice only, as you will remember.

Boy. True.

Soc. And does not this line, reaching from corner to corner, bisect each of these spaces?

Boy. Yes.

Soc. And are there not here four equal lines which contain this space?

Boy. There are.

Soc. Look and see how much this space is.

Boy. I do not understand.

Soc. Has not each interior line cut off half of the four spaces?

Boy. Yes.

Soc. And how many such spaces are there in this section?

Boy. Four.

Soc. And how many in this?

Boy. Two.

Soc. And four is how many times two?

Boy. Twice.

Soc. And this space is of how many feet?

Boy. Of eight feet.

Soc. And from what line do you get this figure?

Boy. From this.

Soc. That is, from the line which extends from corner to corner of the figure of four feet?

Boy. Yes.

Soc. And that is the line which the learned call the diagonal. And if this is the proper name, then you, Meno's slave, are prepared to affirm that the double space is the square of the diagonal?

Boy. Certainly, Socrates.

Soc. What do you say of him, Meno? Were not all these answers given out of his own head?

Men. Yes, they were all his own.

Soc. And yet, as we were just now saying, he did not know?

Men. True.

Soc. But still he had in him those notions of his — had he not?

Men. Yes.

Soc. Then he who does not know may still have true notions of that which he does not know?

Men. He has.

Soc. And at present these notions have just been stirred up in him, as in a dream; but if he were frequently asked the same questions, in different forms, he would know as well as any one at last?

Men. I dare say.

Soc. Without any one teaching him he will recover his knowledge for himself, if he is only asked questions?

Men. Yes.

Soc. And this spontaneous recovery of knowledge in him is recollection?

Men. True.

Soc. And this knowledge which he now has must he not either have acquired or always possessed?

Men. Yes.

Soc. But if he always possessed this knowledge he would always have known; or if he has acquired the knowledge he could not have acquired it in this life, unless he has been taught geometry; for he may be made to do the same with all geometry and every other branch of knowledge. Now, has any one ever taught him all this? You must know about him, if, as you say, he was born and bred in your house.

Men. And I am certain that no one ever did teach him.

Soc. And yet he has the knowledge?

Men. The fact, Socrates, is undeniable.

Soc. But if he did not acquire the knowledge in this life, then he must have had and learned it at some other time?

Men. Clearly he must.

Soc. Which must have been the time when he was not a man?

Men. Yes.

Soc. And if there have been always true thoughts in him, both at the time when he was and was not a man, which only need to be awakened into knowledge by putting questions to him, his soul must have always possessed this knowledge, for he always either was or was not a man?

Men. Obviously.

Soc. And if the truth of all things always existed in the soul, then the soul is immortal. Wherefore be of good cheer, and try to recollect what you do not know, or rather what you do not remember.

Men. I feel, somehow, that I like what you are saying.

Soc. And I, Meno, like what I am saying. Some things I have said of which I am not altogether confident. But that we shall be better and braver and less helpless if we think that we ought to enquire, than we should have been if we indulged in the idle fancy that there was no knowing and no use in seeking to know what we do not know;— that is a theme upon which I am ready to fight, in word and deed, to the utmost of my power.

Men. There again, Socrates, your words seem to me excellent.

Soc. Then, as we are agreed that a man should enquire about that which he does not know, shall you and I make an effort to enquire together into the nature of virtue?

Men. By all means, Socrates. And yet I would much rather return to my original question, Whether in seeking to acquire virtue we should regard it as a thing to be taught, or as a gift of nature, or as coming to men in some other way?

Soc. Had I the command of you as well as of myself, Meno, I would not have enquired whether virtue is given by instruction or not, until we had first ascertained 'what it is.' But as you think only of controlling me who am your slave, and never of controlling yourself,— such being your notion of freedom, I must yield to you, for you are irresistible. And therefore I have now to enquire into the qualities of a thing of which I do not as yet know the nature. At any rate, will you condescend a little, and allow the question ' Whether virtue is given by instruction, or in any other way,' to be argued upon hypothesis? As the geometrician, when he is asked [1] whether a certain triangle is capable of being inscribed in a certain circle [1], will reply : ' I cannot tell you as yet; but I will offer a hypothesis which may assist us in forming a conclusion : If the figure be such that [2] when you have produced a given side of it [2], the given area of the triangle falls short by an area [3] corresponding to the part produced [3], then one consequence follows, and if this is impossible then some other ; and therefore I wish to assume a hypothesis before I tell you whether this triangle is capable of being inscribed in the circle :'— that is a geometrical hypothesis. And we too, as we know not the nature and qualities of virtue, must ask, whether virtue is or is not taught, under a hypothesis : as thus, if virtue is of such a class of mental goods, will it be taught or not? Let the first hypothesis be that virtue is or is not knowledge,— in that case will it be taught or not? or, as we were just now saying, ' remembered '? For there is no use in disputing about the name. But is virtue taught or not? or rather, does not every one see that knowledge alone is taught?

Men. I agree.

Soc. Then if virtue is knowledge, virtue will be taught?

Men Certainly.

[1] Or, whether a certain area is capable of being inscribed as a triangle in a certain circle.

[2] Or, when you apply it to the given line, i. e. the diameter of the circle (αὐτοῦ). [3] Or, similar to the area so applied.

Soc. Then now we have made a quick end of this question: if virtue is of such a nature, it will be taught; and if not, not?

Men. Certainly.

Soc. The next question is, whether virtue is knowledge or of another species?

Men. Yes, that appears to be the question which comes next in order.

Soc. Do we not say that virtue is a good?— This is a hypothesis which is not set aside.

Men. Certainly.

Soc. Now, if there be any sort of good which is distinct from knowledge, virtue may be that good; but if knowledge embraces all good, then we shall be right in thinking that virtue is knowledge?

Men. True.

Soc. And virtue makes us good?

Men. Yes.

Soc. And if we are good, then we are profitable; for all good things are profitable?

Men. Yes.

Soc. Then virtue is profitable?

Men. That is the only inference.

Soc. Then now let us see what are the things which severally profit us. Health and strength, and beauty and wealth — these, and the like of these, we call profitable?

Men. True.

Soc. And yet these things may also sometimes do us harm: would you not think so?

Men. Yes.

Soc. And what is the guiding principle which makes them profitable or the reverse? Are they not profitable when they are rightly used, and hurtful when they are not rightly used?

Men. Certainly.

Soc. Next, let us consider the goods of the soul: they are temperance, justice, courage, quickness of apprehension, memory, magnanimity, and the like?

Men. Surely.

Soc. And such of these as are not knowledge, but of another sort, are sometimes profitable and sometimes hurtful; as, for example, courage wanting prudence, which is only a sort of confidence? When a man has no sense he is harmed by courage, but when he has sense he is profited?

Men. True.

Soc. And the same may be said of temperance and quickness of apprehension; whatever things are learned or done with sense are profitable, but when done without sense they are hurtful?

Men. Very true.

Soc. And in general, all that the soul attempts or endures, when under the guidance of wisdom, ends in happiness; but when she is under the guidance of folly, in the opposite?

Men. That appears to be true.

Soc. If then virtue is a quality of the soul, and is admitted to be profitable, it must be wisdom or prudence, since none of the things of the soul are either profitable or hurtful in themselves, but they are all made profitable or hurtful by the addition of wisdom or of folly; and therefore if virtue is profitable, virtue must be a sort of wisdom or prudence?

Men. I quite agree.

Soc. And the other goods, such as wealth and the like, of which we were just now saying that they are sometimes good and sometimes evil, do not they also become profitable or hurtful, accordingly as the soul guides and uses them rightly or wrongly; just as the things of the soul herself are benefited when under the guidance of wisdom and harmed by folly?

Men. True.

Soc. And the wise soul guides them rightly, and the foolish soul wrongly?

Men. Yes.

Soc. And is not this universally true of human nature? All other things hang upon the soul, and the things of the soul herself hang upon wisdom, if they are to be good; and so wisdom is inferred to be that which profits — and virtue, as we say, is profitable?

Men. Certainly.

Soc. And thus we arrive at the conclusion that virtue is either wholly or partly wisdom?

Men. I think that what you are saying, Socrates, is very true.

Soc. But if this is true, then the good are not by nature good?

Men. I think not.

Soc. If they had been, there would assuredly have been discerners of characters among us who would have known our future great men; and on their showing we should have adopted them, and when we had got them, we should have kept them in the citadel out of the way of harm, and set a stamp upon them far rather than upon a piece of gold, in order that no one might tamper with them; and when they grew up they would have been useful to the state?

Men. Yes, Socrates, that would have been the right way.

Soc. But if the good are not by nature good, are they made good by instruction?

Men. There appears to be no other alternative, Socrates. On the supposition that virtue is knowledge, there can be no doubt that virtue is taught.

Soc. Yes, indeed; but what if the supposition is erroneous?

Men. I certainly thought just now that we were right.

Soc. Yes, Meno; but a principle which has any soundness should stand firm not only just now, but always.

Men. Well; and why are you so slow of heart to believe that knowledge is virtue?

Soc. I will try and tell you why, Meno. I do not retract the assertion that if virtue is knowledge it may be taught; but I fear that I have some reason in doubting whether virtue is knowledge: for consider now and say whether virtue, and not only virtue but anything that is taught, must not have teachers and disciples?

Men. Surely.

Soc. And conversely, may not the art of which neither teachers nor disciples exist be assumed to be incapable of being taught?

Men. True; but do you think that there are no teachers of virtue?

Soc. I have certainly often enquired whether there were any, and taken great pains to find them, and have never succeeded; and many have assisted me in the search, and they were the persons whom I thought the most likely to know. Here at the moment when he is wanted we fortunately have sitting by us Anytus, the very person of whom we should make enquiry; to him then let us repair. In the first place, he is the son of a wealthy and wise father, Anthemion, who acquired his wealth, not by accident or gift, like Ismenias the Theban (who has recently made himself as rich as Polycrates), but by his own skill and industry, and who is a well-conditioned, modest man, not insolent, or over-bearing, or annoying; moreover, this son of his has received a good education, as the Athenian people certainly appear to think, for they choose him to fill the highest offices. And these are the sort of men from whom you are likely to learn whether there are any teachers of virtue, and who they are. Please, Anytus, to help me and your friend Meno in answering our question, Who are the teachers? Consider the matter thus: If we wanted Meno to be a good physician, to whom should we send him? Should we not send him to the physicians?

Any. Certainly.

Soc. Or if we wanted him to be a good cobbler, should we not send him to the cobblers?

Any. Yes.

Soc. And so forth?

Any. Yes.

Soc. Let me trouble you with one more question. When we say that we should be right in sending him to the physicians if we wanted him to be a physician, do we mean that we should be right in sending him to those who profess the art, rather than to those who do not, and to those who demand payment for teaching the art, and profess to teach it to any one who will come and learn? And if these were our reasons, should we not be right in sending him?

Any. Yes.

Soc. And might not the same be said of flute-playing, and of the other arts? Would a man who wanted to make another a flute-player refuse to send him to those who profess to teach the art for money, and be plaguing other persons to give him instruction, who are not professed teachers and who never had a single disciple in that branch of knowledge which he wishes him to acquire — would not such conduct be the height of folly?

Any. Yes, by Zeus, and of ignorance too.

Soc. Very good. And now you are in a position to advise with me about my friend Meno. He has been telling me, Anytus, that he desires to attain that kind of wisdom and virtue by which men order the state or the house, and honour their parents, and know when to receive and when to send away citizens and strangers, as a good man should. Now, to whom should he go in order that he may learn this virtue? Does not the previous argument imply clearly that we should send him to those who profess and avouch that they are the common teachers of all Hellas, and are ready to impart instruction to any one who likes, at a fixed price?

Any. Whom do you mean, Socrates?

Soc. You surely know, do you not, Anytus, that these are the people whom mankind call Sophists?

Any. By Heracles, Socrates, forbear! I only hope that no friend or kinsman or acquaintance of mine, whether citizen or stranger, will ever be so mad as to allow himself to be corrupted by them; for they are a manifest pest and corrupting influence to those who have to do with them.

Soc. What, Anytus? Of all the people who profess that they know how to do men good, do you mean to say that these are the only ones who not only do them no good, but positively corrupt those who are entrusted to them, and in return for this disservice have the face to demand money? Indeed, I cannot believe you; for I know of a single man, Protagoras, who made more out of his craft than the illustrious Pheidias, who created such noble works, or any ten other statuaries. How could that be? A mender of old shoes, or patcher up of clothes, who made the shoes or clothes worse than he received them, could not have remained thirty days undetected, and would very soon have starved; whereas during more than forty years, Protagoras was corrupting all Hellas, and sending his disciples from him worse than he received them, and he was never found out. For, if I am not mistaken, he was about seventy years old at his death, forty of which were spent in the practice of his profession; and during all that time he had a good reputation, which to this day he retains: and not only Protagoras, but many others are well spoken of; some who lived before him, and others who are still living. Now, when you say that they deceived and corrupted the youth, are they to be supposed to have corrupted them consciously or unconsciously? Can those who were deemed by many to be the wisest men of Hellas have been out of their minds?

Any. Out of their minds! No, Socrates; the young men who gave their money to them were out of their minds, and their relations and guardians who entrusted their youth to the care of these men were still more out of their minds, and most of all, the cities who allowed them to come in, and did not drive them out, citizen and stranger alike.

Soc. Has any of the Sophists wronged you, Anytus? What makes you so angry with them?

Any. No, indeed, neither I nor any of my belongings has ever had, nor would I suffer them to have, anything to do with them.

Soc. Then you are entirely unacquainted with them?

Any. And I have no wish to be acquainted.

Soc. Then, my dear friend, how can you know whether a thing is good or bad of which you are wholly ignorant?

Any. Quite well; I am sure that I know what manner of men these are, whether I am acquainted with them or not.

Soc. You must be a diviner, Anytus, for I really cannot make out, judging from your own words, how, if you are not acquainted with them, you know about them. But I am not enquiring of you who are the teachers who will corrupt Meno (let them be, if you please, the Sophists); I only ask you to tell him who there is in this great city who will teach him how to become eminent in the virtues which I was just now describing. He is the friend of your family, and you will oblige him.

Any. Why do you not tell him yourself?

Soc. I have told him whom I supposed to be the teachers of these things; but I learn from you that I am utterly at fault, and I dare say that you are right. And now I wish that you, on your part, would tell me to whom among the Athenians he should go. Whom would you name?

Any. Why single out individuals? Any Athenian gentleman, taken at random, if he will mind him, will do far more good to him than the Sophists.

Soc. And did those gentlemen grow of themselves; and without having been taught by any one, were they nevertheless able to teach others that which they had never learned themselves?

Any. I imagine that they learned of the previous generation of gentlemen. Have there not been many good men in this city?

Soc. Yes, certainly, Anytus; and many good statesmen also there always have been and there are still, in the city of Athens. But the question is whether they were also good teachers of their own virtue;— not whether there are, or have been, good men in this part of the world, but whether virtue can be taught, is the question which we have been discussing. Now, do we mean to say that the good men of our own and of other times knew how to impart to others that virtue which they had themselves; or is virtue a thing incapable of being communicated or imparted by one man to another? That is the question which I and Meno have been arguing. Look at the matter in your own way: Would you not admit that Themistocles was a good man?

Any. Certainly; no man better.

Soc. And must not he then have been a good teacher, if any man ever was a good teacher, of his own virtue?

Any. Yes, certainly,— if he wanted to be so.

Soc. But would he not have wanted? He would, at any rate, have desired to make his own son a good man and a gentleman; he could not have been jealous of him, or have intentionally abstained from imparting to him his own virtue. Did you never hear that he made his son Cleophantus a famous horseman; and had him taught to stand upright on horseback and hurl a javelin, and to do many other marvellous things; and in anything which could be learned from a master he was well trained? Have you not heard from our elders of him?

Any. I have.

Soc. Then no one could say that his son showed any want of capacity?

Any. Very likely not.

Soc. But did any one, old or young, ever say in your hearing that Cleophantus, son of Themistocles, was a wise or good man, as his father was?

Any. I have certainly never heard any one say so.

Soc. And if virtue could have been taught, would his father Themistocles have sought to train him in these minor accomplishments, and allowed him who, as you must remember, was his own son, to be no better than his neighbours in those qualities in which he himself excelled?

Any. Indeed, indeed, I think not.

Soc. Here was a teacher of virtue whom you admit to be among the best men of the past. Let us take another,— Aristides, the son of Lysimachus: would you not acknowledge that he was a good man?

Any. To be sure I should.

Soc. And did not he train his son Lysimachus better than any other Athenian in all that could be done for him by the help of masters? But what has been the result? Is he a bit better than any other mortal? He is an acquaintance of yours, and you see what he is like. There is Pericles, again, magnificent in his wisdom; and he, as you are aware, had two sons, Paralus and Xanthippus.

Any. I know.

Soc. And you know, also, that he taught them to be unrivalled horsemen, and had them trained in music and gymnastics and all sorts of arts — in these respects they were on a level with the best — and had he no wish to make good men of them? Nay, he must have wished it. But virtue, as I suspect, could not be taught. And that you may not suppose the incompetent teachers to be only the meaner sort of Athenians and few in number, remember again that Thucydides had two sons, Melesias and Stephanus, whom, besides giving them a good education in other things, he trained in wrestling, and they were the best wrestlers in Athens: one of them he committed to the care of Xanthias, and the other of Eudorus, who had the reputation of being the most celebrated wrestlers of that day. Do you remember them?

Any. I have heard of them.

Soc. Now, can there be a doubt that Thucydides, whose children were taught things for which he had to spend money, would have taught them to be good men, which would have cost him nothing, if virtue could have been taught? Will you reply that he was a mean man, and had not many friends among the Athenians and allies? Nay, but he was of a great family, and a man of influence at Athens and in all Hellas, and, if virtue could have been taught, he would have found out some Athenian or foreigner who would have made good men of his sons, if he could not himself spare the time from cares of state. Once more, I suspect, friend Anytus, that virtue is not a thing which can be taught?

Any. Socrates, I think that you are too ready to speak evil of men: and, if you will take my advice, I would recommend you to be careful. Perhaps there is no city in which it is not easier to do men harm than to do them good, and this is certainly the case at Athens, as I believe that you know.

Soc. O Meno, I think that Anytus is in a rage. And he may well be in a rage, for he thinks, in the first place, that I am defaming these gentlemen; and in the second place, he is of opinion that he is one of them himself. But some day he will know what is the meaning of defamation, and if he ever does, he will forgive me. Meanwhile I will return to you, Meno; for I suppose that there are gentlemen in your region too?

Men. Certainly there are.

Soc. And are they willing to teach the young? and do they profess to be teachers? and do they agree that virtue is taught?

Men. No indeed, Socrates, they are anything but agreed; you may hear them saying at one time that virtue can be taught, and then again the reverse.

Soc. Can we call those teachers who do not acknowledge the possibility of their own vocation?

Men. I think not, Socrates.

Soc. And what do you think of these Sophists, who are the only professors? Do they seem to you to be teachers of virtue?

Men. I often wonder, Socrates, that Gorgias is never heard promising to teach virtue: and when he hears others promising he only laughs at them; but he thinks that men should be taught to speak.

Soc. Then do you not think that the Sophists are teachers?

Men. I cannot tell you, Socrates; like the rest of the world,

I am in doubt, and sometimes I think that they are teachers and sometimes not.

Soc. And are you aware that not you only and other politicians have doubts whether virtue can be taught or not, but that Theognis the poet says the very same thing?

Men. Where does he say so?

Soc. In these elegiac verses[1] :—

' Eat and drink and sit with the mighty, and make yourself agreeable to them ; for from the good you will learn what is good, but if you mix with the bad you will lose the intelligence which you already have.'

Do you observe that here he seems to imply that virtue can be taught?

Men. Clearly.

Soc. But in some other verses he shifts about and says[2] :—

' If understanding could be created and put into a man, then they ' [who were able to perform this feat] ' would have obtained great rewards.'

And again :—

' Never would a bad son have sprung from a good sire, for he would have heard the voice of instruction ; but not by teaching will you ever make a bad man into a good one.'

And this, as you may remark, is a contradiction of the other.

Men. Clearly.

Soc. And is there anything else of which the professors are affirmed not only not to be teachers of others, but to be ignorant themselves, and bad at the knowledge of that which they are professing to teach? or is there anything about which even the acknowledged 'gentlemen' are sometimes saying that 'this thing can be taught,' and sometimes the opposite? Can you say that they are teachers in any true sense whose ideas are in such confusion?

Men. I should say, certainly not.

Soc. But if neither the Sophists nor the gentlemen are teachers, clearly there can be no other teachers?

Men. No.

Soc. And if there are no teachers, neither are there disciples?

Men. Agreed.

[1] Theog. 33 ff. [2] Theog. 435 ff.

Soc. And we have admitted that a thing cannot be taught of which there are neither teachers nor disciples?

Men. We have.

Soc. And there are no teachers of virtue to be found anywhere?

Men. There are not.

Soc. And if there are no teachers, neither are there scholars?

Men. That, I think, is true.

Soc. Then virtue cannot be taught?

Men. Not if we are right in our view. But I cannot believe, Socrates, that there are no good men: And if there are, how did they come into existence?

Soc. I am afraid, Meno, that you and I are not good for much, and that Gorgias has been as poor an educator of you as Prodicus has been of me. Certainly we shall have to look to ourselves, and try to find some one who will help in some way or other to improve us. This I say, because I observe that in the previous discussion none of us remarked that right and good action is possible to man under other guidance than that of knowledge (ἐπιστήμη) ;— and indeed if this be denied, there is no seeing how there can be any good men at all.

Men. How do you mean, Socrates?

Soc. I mean that good men are necessarily useful or profitable. Were we not right in admitting this? It must be so.

Men. Yes.

Soc. And in supposing that they will be useful only if they are true guides to us of action — there we were also right?

Men. Yes.

Soc. But when we said that a man cannot be a good guide unless he have knowledge (φρόνησις), in this we were wrong.

Men. What do you mean by the word 'right'?

Soc. I will explain. If a man knew the way to Larisa, or anywhere else, and went to the place and led others thither, would he not be a right and good guide?

Men. Certainly.

Soc. And a person who had a right opinion about the way, but had never been and did not know, might be a good guide also, might he not?

Men. Certainly.

Soc. And while he has true opinion about that which the other knows, he will be just as good a guide if he thinks the truth, as he who knows the truth?

Men. Exactly.

Soc. Then true opinion is as good a guide to correct action as knowledge; and that was the point which we omitted in our speculation about the nature of virtue, when we said that knowledge only is the guide of right action; whereas there is also right opinion.

Men. True.

Soc. Then right opinion is not less useful than knowledge?

Men. The difference, Socrates, is only that he who has knowledge will always be right; but he who has right opinion will sometimes be right, and sometimes not.

Soc. What do you mean? Can he be wrong who has right opinion, so long as he has right opinion?

Men. I admit the cogency of your argument, and therefore, Socrates, I wonder that knowledge should be preferred to right opinion — or why they should ever differ.

Soc. And shall I explain this wonder to you?

Men. Do tell me.

Soc. You would not wonder if you had ever observed the images of Daedalus[1]; but perhaps you have not got them in your country?

Men. What have they to do with the question?

Soc. Because they require to be fastened in order to keep them, and if they are not fastened they will play truant and run away.

Men. Well, what of that?

Soc. I mean to say that they are not very valuable possessions if they are at liberty, for they will walk off like runaway slaves; but when fastened, they are of great value, for they are really beautiful works of art. Now this is an illustration of the nature of true opinions: while they abide with us they are beautiful and, fruitful, but they run away out of the human soul, and do not remain long, and therefore they are not of much value until they are fastened by the tie of the cause; and this fastening of them, friend **Meno,**

[1] Cp. Euthyphro 11 B.

is recollection, as you and I have agreed to call it. But when they are bound, in the first place, they have the nature of knowledge; and, in the second place, they are abiding. And this is why knowledge is more honourable and excellent than true opinion, because fastened by a chain.

Men. What you are saying, Socrates, seems to be very like the truth.

Soc. I too speak rather in ignorance; I only conjecture. And yet that knowledge differs from true opinion is no matter of conjecture with me. There are not many things which I profess to know, but this is most certainly one of them.

Men. Yes, Socrates; and you are quite right in saying so.

Soc. And am I' not also right in saying that true opinion leading the way perfects action quite as well as knowledge?

Men. There again, Socrates, I think that you are right.

Soc. Then right opinion is not a whit inferior to knowledge, or less useful in action; nor is the man who has right opinion inferior to him who has knowledge?

Men. True.

Soc. And surely the good man has been acknowledged by us to be useful?

Men. Yes.

Soc. Seeing then that men become good and useful to states, not only because they have knowledge, but because they have right opinion, and that neither knowledge nor right opinion is given to man by nature or acquired by him — (do you imagine either of them to be given by nature?

Men. Not I.)

Soc. Then if they are not given by nature, neither are the good by nature good?

Men. Certainly not.

Soc. And nature being excluded, then came the question whether virtue is acquired by teaching?

Men. Yes.

Soc. If virtue was wisdom [or knowledge], then, as we thought, it was taught?

Men. Yes.

Soc. And if it was taught it was wisdom?

Men. Certainly.

Soc. And if there were teachers, it might be taught; and if there were no teachers, not?

Men. True.

Soc. But surely we acknowledged that there were no teachers of virtue?

Men. Yes.

Soc. Then we acknowledged that it was not taught, and was not wisdom?

Men. Certainly.

Soc. And yet we admitted that it was a good?

Men. Yes.

Soc. And the right guide is useful and good?

Men. Certainly.

Soc. And the only right guides are knowledge and true opinion — these are the guides of man; for things which happen by chance are not under the guidance of man: but the guides of man are true opinion and knowledge.

Men. I think so too.

Soc. But if virtue is not taught, neither is virtue knowledge.

Men. Clearly not.

Soc. Then of two good and useful things, one, which is knowledge, has been set aside, and cannot be supposed to be our guide in political life.

Men. I think not.

Soc. And therefore not by any wisdom, and not because they were wise, did Themistocles and those others of whom Anytus spoke govern states. This was the reason why they were unable to make others like themselves — because their virtue was not grounded on knowledge.

Men. That is probably true, Socrates.

Soc. But if not by knowledge, the only alternative which remains is that statesmen must have guided states by right opinion, which is in politics what divination is in religion; for diviners and also prophets say many things truly, but they know not what they say.

Men. So I believe.

Soc. And may we not, Meno, truly call those men 'divine' who, having no understanding, yet succeed in many a grand deed and word?

Men. Certainly.

Soc. Then we shall also be right in calling divine those whom we were just now speaking of as diviners and prophets, including the whole tribe of poets. Yes, and statesmen above all may be said to be divine and illumined, being inspired and possessed of God, in which condition they say many grand things, not knowing what they say.

Men. Yes.

Soc. And the women too, Meno, call good men divine — do they not? and the Spartans, when they praise a good man, say 'that he is a divine man.'

Men. And I think, Socrates, that they are right; although very likely our friend Anytus may take offence at the word.

Soc. I do not care; as for Anytus, there will be another opportunity of talking with him. To sum up our enquiry — the result seems to be, if we are at all right in our view, that virtue is neither natural nor acquired, but an instinct given by God to the virtuous. Nor is the instinct accompanied by reason, unless there may be supposed to be among statesmen some one who is capable of educating statesmen. And if there be such an one, he may be said to be among the living what Homer says that Tiresias was among the dead, 'he alone has understanding; but the rest are flitting shades;' and he and his virtue in like manner will be a reality among shadows.

Men. That is excellent, Socrates.

Soc. Then, Meno, the conclusion is that virtue comes to the virtuous by the gift of God. But we shall never know the certain truth until, before asking how virtue is given, we enquire into the actual nature of virtue. I fear that I must go away, but do you, now that you are persuaded yourself, persuade our friend Anytus. And do not let him be so exasperated; if you can conciliate him, you will have done good service to the Athenian people.

The Platonic Method *was composed in Linotype Fairfield, with Michelangelo display type, by* The Composing Room, Inc., New York. *The entire book was printed by offset lithography. Typography and binding design by Joan Stoliar.*